A POSSESSORY ESTATES
AND
FUTURE INTERESTS PRIMER
Second Edition

By

Peter T. Wendel

Professor of Law
Pepperdine University School of Law

THOMSON

WEST

Mat #16366293

COPYRIGHT © 1996 WEST PUBLISHING CO.
© 2005 Thomson/West
      610 Opperman Drive
      P.O. Box 64526
      St. Paul, MN 55164–0526
      1–800–328–9352

Printed in the United States of America

ISBN 0–314–23819–0

 *TEXT IS PRINTED ON 10% POST CONSUMER RECYCLED PAPER*

To my wife, Gerri,

for agreeing share our life estates,

and for bearing our four lovely remainders:

Carolyn, Paul, John and Kristin

PREFACE

A complete study of the abstract beauty of possessory estates and future interests is best left to its own upper level course. The basic Property course and/or Wills & Trusts course is incomplete, however, without a two to three week introduction to the basic principles and combinations of possessory estates and future interests. This material provides just such an introduction.

Such an expedited coverage of such a complex and extensive area of law, however, inherently requires simplifications and generalizations. As you become more familiar with the material, you will begin to see the myriad of possible combinations of possessory estates and future interests. Although the material covers some of these combinations in footnotes, such complex combinations are generally beyond the scope of the introductory coverage. The goal here is to understand the basic principles and combinations of possessory estate and future interests necessary to understand the material covered in most Property courses and/or Wills & Trusts courses.

I wish to express my thanks and appreciation to my colleagues, Dean Charles I. Nelson, for his contributions to the first edition of this book, and Prof. Shelley Saxer, for her thorough reading of the manuscript and her excellent comments and criticism. In addition, I would like to thank my research assistants, Ms. Theona Zhordania-Taat, Ms. Jennifer Black, and Mr. Jean-Paul Le Clercq, for their invaluable research assistance and proofreading. And finally, I would like to thank all of the Pepperdine students over the years who have endured my Property class and my experiments with how best to present the material. Their honest and thoughtful reactions to my different ideas helped to formulate this latest approach. In many respects this book is the product of years of shared learning process that naturally occurs in the classroom, and their contributions make this book much better. I hope that you find it useful in your studies.

Peter Wendel

Malibu, California
March, 2005

Table of Contents

Chapter 1
INTRODUCTION

Chapter 2
THE FEE SIMPLE ABSOLUTE

Chapter 3
THE FEE SIMPLE DEFEASIBLES

Chapter 4
THE FINITE ESTATES

Chapter 5
REMAINDERS: VESTED vs. CONTINGENT

Chapter 6
ALTERNATIVE APPROACH FOR ANALYZING CONVEYANCES – LEAD WITH THE PARTIES

Chapter 7
VARIATIONS ON THE EXECUTORY INTERESTS

Chapter 8
DISTINGUISHNG THE CONDITION PRECEDENT FROM THE CONDITION SUBSEQUENT FROM THE DIVESTING CONDITION

Chapter 9
ONE LAST SET OF ESTATES:
LIFE ESTATES DEFEASIBLE

Chapter 10
MISCELLANEOUS COMMON LAW RULES
REGULATING CONVEYANCES

Chapter 11
CLASS GIFTS

Chapter 12
THE RULE AGAINST PERPETUITIES

APPENDIX A
ANSWERS TO PROBLEM SETS

Chapter 1

INTRODUCTION

I. OVERVIEW

A. INTRODUCTION

O[1] is the owner of Greenacres, a 200 acre farm:

```
┌──────────────────────────────────────────┐
│                                          │
│                                          │
│              GREENACRES                  │
│                                          │
│                                          │
└──────────────────────────────────────────┘
```

O decides she wants to give Greenacres to A and B. She comes to you for advice on how she can divide Greenacres between them. One way she could divide Greenacres is simply to split it in half, giving 100 acres to A and 100 acres to B. But just as property can be divided physically, property rights can also be divided temporally - over time.

The study of the temporal division of property interests is the study of possessory estates and future interests. The party who currently holds the right to take *actual* possession of the property *right now* holds the **possessory estate;** the party who currently holds the right to take *actual* possession of the property *in the future* (when the possessory estate ends), holds the **future interest.**[2] For example, O could give Greenacres "to A for

---

[1] "O" is the Owner's abbreviated name. Anytime you see a capital letter in a conveyance, such as O or A, B, C, etc., assume the capital letter is the abbreviation of a personal name. In this example, O could be Olivia Olinich, A could be Abigail Anderson, and B could be Betty Booqu. Assume each party is alive at the time of the conveyance.

[2] Both possessory estates and future interests are **present property rights** in that the holder **presently** has the right to possess the land. The right to possess the land may be immediate, in which case the interest is a possessory interest, or it may be the right to possess the property in the future, in which case the interest is a future interest; in either case, the holder **presently** owns that right. Possession is not a mere hope, it is a right. In

life, then to B and her heirs." [3] A would hold the possessory estate (the right to possess Greenacres right now), and B would hold the future interest (the right to possess Greenacres in the future - upon A's death). This is but one example of how O could split the property temporally between A and B. There are many different ways a property interest can be split over time. The different possible combinations of temporal estates, and how such estates are created, are the essence of the law of possessory estates and future interests.

B. HISTORICAL ROOTS

Possessory estate and future interests were first created during early common law in response to historical conditions and rules which existed at that time. Although many of these conditions and rules no longer exist, the terminology and basic combinations of estates which developed then generally remain intact today. Analytically, however, it is possible to learn possessory estates and future interests without a detailed examination of their historical roots. This material will refer to the historical origins of the possessory estate and future interest scheme only to the limited extent that it aids in understanding the present terms and schemes.

C. INSTRUMENTS USED TO CREATE

Possessory estates and future interests can be created in a number of different written instruments. The simplest way to create the interests is in a deed, in which case they are known as *legal* possessory estates and future interests. Possessory estates and future interests are best understood, however, in the context of a trust. In a trust, the trustee holds legal title and the trust beneficiaries hold the equitable interest in the trust property. Invariably the trust beneficiaries' interests are split over time into some combination of possessory estates and future interests. [4]

---

the case of the future interest, full enjoyment of the right is delayed, but the right to possess the land in the future is still a present right.

[3] Although possessory estates and future interests can be created in either personal property or real property, historically possessory estates and future interests were used primarily with real property. For many students, it is conceptually easier to think about the system of possessory estates and future interests in the context of real property. For that reason, the hypotheticals generally will assume the property being conveyed is real property. It is recommended that you use this mindset as well in thinking about possessory estates and future interests.

[4] For example, upon learning that he had terminal cancer, the patient established a trust for his benefit for the remainder of his life, then for the benefit of his wife for her life, and upon her death, the property is to be distributed outright to his children equally.

Because trust beneficiaries hold the equitable interest in a trust, they hold *equitable* possessory estates and future interests (created in a trust) as opposed to legal possessory estates and future interests (created in a deed typically). Overlapping the law of trusts onto the law of possessory estates and future interests, however, only further complicates the already challenging task of learning the latter.[5] To minimize the degree of difficulty associated with learning the basics of possessory estates and future interests, the material will assume, for the most part, that the conveyance is in the form of a deed and creates a legal possessory estate and future interest. In the real world, however, it is extremely rare to see possessory estates and future interests outside of a trust.

II. T HE ANALYTICAL SCHEME

Although it is important to know how to create (i.e., how to draft) possessory estates and future interests, the introductory coverage to possessory estates and future interests focuses primarily on how to construe possessory estates and future interests drafted by someone else.[6] In construing a conveyance,[7] there will be only one possessory estate, but there can be more than one future interest. Construing possessory estates and future interests involves properly analyzing which possessory estate has been created and properly analyzing which future interest or interests have been created.

A. POSSESSORY ESTATES

Proper analysis of the possessory estate involves two steps: (1) identify **who** holds the possessory estate, and (2) identify **which possessory estate it is** based upon its duration. Different possessory estates last for

---

[5] Accordingly, most introductory coverages focus on *legal* possessory estates and future interests to minimize the degree of difficulty. In reality, however, legal possessory estates and future interests are rare and are to be discouraged. The disadvantages associated with legal future interests in land are so numerous that in England, the homeland of possessory estates and future interests, they are now prohibited as a general rule. Only equitable possessory estates future interests are permitted. EDWARD H. RABIN ET AL., FUNDAMENTALS OF MODERN REAL PROPERTY LAW 191 (4th ed., Foundation Press 2000).

[6] You should keep in mind, however, how you would *create* such possessory estates and future interests. Knowing the proper way to create the estates facilitates construing them.

[7] A conveyance is a generic term used to describe the different ways property can be transferred from one party to another: (1) either for consideration (a sale) or as a gift (a donative transfer), and (2) either inter vivos (while the grantor/transferor is alive) or testamentary (at the time of the grantor's/transferor's death).

different periods of time. In theory a *fee simple absolute* lasts forever, while a *life estate* lasts only for the life of the grantee. Each possessory estate has its own **"words of limitation"** which indicate its **duration** and which *must* be used to create that possessory estate. In analyzing a possessory estate, the key is to focus on the express language of the conveyance to identify which words of limitation are used. The words of limitation used will determine the duration of the estate, and the duration of the estate will help determine which possessory estate has been created.

B. FUTURE INTERESTS

Proper analysis of each future interest involves three steps: (1) identify **who** holds the future interest; (2) identify **which future interest the party holds**; and (3) indicate **the duration of the future interest**. Compared to the analysis of a possessory estate, analysis of a future interest involves the added step of identifying which future interest the party holds. Which future interest the party holds depends on (a) which possessory estate it follows, and (b) who holds the future interest. Unlike the possessory estates, the name of the future interest does *not* indicate *how long* the party will have the right to possession once the future interest becomes possessory. That is why for each future interest, there must also be a possessory estate. Identifying the duration of the future interest is the same as identifying any other possessory estate. The express *words of limitation* in the clause creating the future interest is the best evidence of the possessory estate the future interest holds (the duration of the future interest once it becomes possessory).

C. THE ANALYTICAL KEYS

Possessory estates and future interests are rather abstract.[8] The key is to focus on the **terminology** (at times it will seem like a foreign language), the requisite **words of limitation** necessary to create the different estates, and the different possible combinations of possessory estates and future interests. Analytically the best way to master possessory estates and future interests is to (1) group them into the different possible **categories of possessory estates**, and (2) know how to distinguish the different possible combinations within each category. The material will take you through this approach step by step, and

---

[8] So abstract that parts of the prior paragraphs no doubt seemed incomprehensible. Do not worry if you do not fully understand the material so far. The rest of the book breaks down these sentences into digestible components and gives examples that simplify the material to the point where you will be able to understand it fully.

when you are done, you will understand how to analyze possessory estates and future interests. In addition, practice makes perfect. The more possessory estate and future interest problems you do, the better you will get at analyzing conveyances.

Chapter 2

THE FEE SIMPLE ABSOLUTE

I. OVERVIEW

There are three core *categories* of possessory estates: the fee simple absolute, the fee simple defeasibles, and the finite estates. The defining characteristic of the first category of possessory estates is that the estate, the *fee simple absolute, in theory, lasts forever.* The fee simple absolute (or "the fee simple" as it is also known) is by far the most important and most prevalent possessory estate. It is so important that it is in a category all by itself.

II. THE FEE SIMPLE ABSOLUTE

A. THE NATURE OF THE ESTATE

The fee simple absolute is the benchmark estate against which all other possessory estates are compared and analyzed.[9] You actually already know this estate, although you probably do not know it by its technical name. Return to the opening hypothetical. The material began by stating that "O is the owner of Greenacres, ..." When you read that sentence, you probably did not even stop to think about what the material meant when it said O "owns" Greenacres. When someone "owns" a piece of property, without any qualification, what does that mean? From a possessory estates and future interests standpoint, it means that O holds the property in **fee simple absolute.** In theory, O has the right to possess the property forever (if O could live that long). **There is no future interest.** No one presently has the right to possess the property in the future. There is **no inherent condition or restriction** limiting how O can use the property.[10] While O is alive, O has the right to transfer the property freely to whomever he or she

---

[9] CORNELIUS J. MOYNIHAN, INTRODUCTION TO THE LAW OF REAL PROPERTY 26 (1962).

[10] RESTATEMENT (FIRST) OF PROPERTY §§ 14-15 (1936) [hereinafter PROPERTY RESTATEMENT].

wishes.[11]

Although in theory O has the right to possess the land forever, in reality O will die at some point. Upon O's death, with a fee simple absolute, he or she can devise the property as he or she wishes.[12] In the event he or she fails to devise the property, it will pass to his or her heirs.[13] The fee simple absolute is the largest, most complete estate a person can hold.

B. THE WORDS OF PURCHASE

Having established the temporal duration of the fee simple absolute (in theory it lasts forever), and the scope of the interest (there are no conditions or limitations on O's right to use or transfer it), the last key is how to create (and thus recognize) a fee simple absolute.[14] Assume O owns Greenacres and wants to transfer it to A in fee simple absolute. Obviously the instrument of transfer must say "to A" to indicate the party to whom the property is being transferred. These words constitute the **words of**

---

[11] The ability to transfer property inter vivos (while the grantor is alive), either by gift or for consideration, is also known as the right to *alienate* the property.

[12] When a person dies, there are two basic ways in which property rights, which survive the decedent, may be passed on to other individuals. If the decedent dies with a will (dies "testate"), the will may direct to whom the decedent's property goes (the decedent/testator is said to "devise" the property to a devisee or beneficiary). When the decedent dies without a will (dies "intestate"), the property passes to the decedent's heirs pursuant to the state's intestate distribution scheme. The recipients (the heirs) "inherit" the property.

[13] The material just said that there is no future interest and yet now it says that upon O's death, O has the right to devise it to whomever he or she wishes, and if he or she fails to devise it, his or her heirs will inherit it. Does that mean that one or the other party *must* have a future interest? No. While O is alive, the heirs apparent (the parties who *think* they will receive the owner's property when he or she dies) have a mere **expectancy**, but no property interest (no present right to possess the property in the future). Any interest the heirs have can be defeated by O simply executing a will which devises the property to someone else or by conveying the property *inter vivos* to someone else. Likewise, devisees under a will have no property interest until the testator dies (no present right to possess the property in the future); all they have is an expectancy. A future interest is a present **right** to possess the property in the future. Neither an heir nor a devisee has a present right while O is alive; hence, no future interest.

[14] As with all drafting, there is the proper terminology to create the desired end, and there is the issue of how an instrument should be construed if the drafter fails to use the proper terminology. The material will focus on, and presume, proper drafting technique based on the traditional common law approach. Later the material will cover in more detail the modern trend changes to the common law drafting principles, and the default rules when improper drafting is used. *See* discussion *infra* Ch. 4, II, A.

purchase[15] – the words in the conveyance which indicate to whom the property is being transferred.[16] But inasmuch as property interests can be divided temporally, we also need to know the **duration** of the property interest being transferred.

C. THE WORDS OF LIMITATION

One of the keys to identifying which possessory estate is being created is to focus on the duration of the estate. The express words in the conveyance which indicate the duration of the estate are called the **words of limitation**.[17] Common law was very demanding in requiring use of the appropriate words of limitation. The words of limitation, or "drafting words," necessary at common law to create a fee simple absolute were **"and her heirs."**[18] Combining the words of purchase ("to A") with the words of limitation ("and her heirs"),[19] the conveyance should be expressed as follows:

EXAMPLE 1

O →[20] To A and her heirs.

---

[15] Although the phrase is "words of **purchase**," there is no requirement that the grantee pay consideration. The grantee can take by gift. The phrase merely indicates **to whom** the property is being transferred via a written instrument (because of the written instrument requirement, there are no words of purchase when the property passes by inheritance, but there are when the property passes under the terms of a will). MOYNIHAN, *supra* note 9, at 28.

[16] *Id.*

[17] *Id.*

[18] Or, if the recipient were a male, "and *his* heirs." The magic word is "heir." Other words (such as "children") create ambiguity as to whether a joint interest was intended for O and her children, giving the children a present interest, or whether the children were intended to have a future interest after O's death, or whether the children were to have no interest and the grantor intended a fee simple absolute. The operative word of limitation is "heir" to indicate a fee simple absolute under the traditional common law approach.

[19] The "words of limitation" refers to the special drafting words necessary to create each possessory estate. There are special words of limitation for each possessory estate. The particular words of limitation necessary to create a fee simple absolute at common law, "and his/her heirs," are also known as the "words of general inheritance." PROPERTY RESTATEMENT, *supra* note 10, at § 27, cmt. c.

[20] The small arrow indicates that a property interest is being conveyed by the grantor to one or more grantees. Depending on the facts, the conveyance could take place inter vivos (typically by a deed) or testamentary (upon O's death). A testamentary transfer typically is by a will. (Although a will is executed inter vivos, it is not effective until the person (the testator) dies – which makes the transfers under the will testamentary transfers.) If the facts do not indicate otherwise, assume that the conveyance is an inter vivos conveyance.

Notice the order of the words. First, the words of purchase ("to A"), which indicate to whom the property interest is being transferred; and then the words of limitation ("and her heirs"), which indicate the estate being transferred:

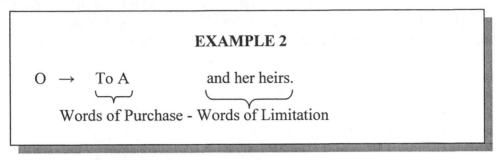

EXAMPLE 2

O → To A and her heirs.

Words of Purchase - Words of Limitation

This is the basic sequencing of the words of purchase/words of limitation of every estate, be it possessory or future.

D. ANALYZING THE POSSESSORY ESTATE

While the above example examines how to *draft* a fee simple absolute, from a student's perspective the norm is that you will be given a conveyance and you will be asked to *identify* the possessory estate and future interests created. With respect to the possessory estate, the analysis is a two step process: (1) identify **who** holds the possessory estate (find the words of purchase "to X ..."), and (2) indicate **which possessory estate** the party holds (find the **words of limitation** which indicate the **duration** of the estate). That is the analytical scheme that you should apply to every estate, in every conveyance, that you are asked to analyze.

The conveyance of a fee simple absolute from O to A can be diagrammed on a time line:[21]

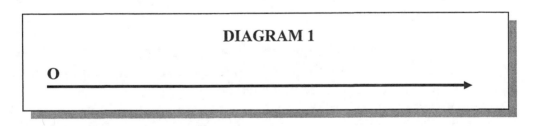

DIAGRAM 1

O ——————————————————→

---

[21] All possessory estates and future interests can be diagrammed temporally by using a time line. Being able to "visualize" possessory estates and future interests helps some students, particularly when they are first introduced to the estates.

The arrow represents a time line which stretches out to the right into the future theoretically for eternity. For each conveyance, you should assume that O, the original owner, holds the property in fee simple absolute unless told otherwise. Just as in theory a fee simple absolute lasts forever, so too does the time line arrow O holds. If and when O transfers the property, that is indicated on the time line by a cross line towards the left end of the arrow:

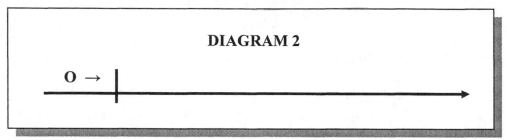

This cross line (and the smaller arrow just to the left of it) indicates the point in time when O conveyed the property. The part of the time line to the right of the cross line indicates how O conveyed the property in terms of the possessory estate and future interest(s) created. If there are no other lines to the right of the "time of conveyance" cross line, just the uninterrupted time line stretching out to the right, that indicates that the transferee/grantee[22] has the right to hold the property in theory for eternity. The grantee holds a fee simple absolute. For each property interest conveyed, to the right of the cross line write: (1) the name of the grantee, and (2) the name of the property interest he or she received. For example, the complete diagram for the conveyance "To A and her heirs" is:

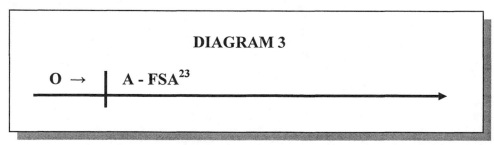

O conveyed a fee simple absolute to A. Because a fee simple absolute lasts forever, A receives the rest of the time line.[24]

---

[22] These terms are synonymous for purposes of this material. They indicate to whom the property interest has been conveyed.

[23] When diagramming conveyances, you may find it easier to abbreviate the different possessory estates and future interests.

[24] For each conveyance, you need to account for the whole time line from the time of

In analyzing conveyances, the words of purchase ("to A") are relatively easy to identify and analyze - all that really changes is the identity of the recipient. Accordingly, your focus should be on the words immediately following the words of purchase – those words typically constitute the words of limitation (for example – "and her heirs"). The words of limitation indicate the duration of the estate created, which in turn indicate which possessory estate is being created. To master the scheme of possessory estates and future interests you must memorize and master the words of limitation necessary to create the different basic estates. The words of limitation which indicate a fee simple absolute are "and her heirs/and his heirs."

The fee simple absolute is the most complete estate a person can hold and it is the estate against which all the other possessory estates should be compared.

III. THE MODERN TREND DRAFTING APPROACH

The modern trend presumes that a grantor intends to convey all that he or she owns in the absence of express words of limitation indicating the intent to limit the estate being conveyed.[25] Under the modern trend, a grantor need not use the technical words of limitation "and her heirs/and her heirs" to convey a fee simple absolute (assuming that is what the grantor owned at the time of the conveyance). Any words of limitation that express the intent to convey a fee simple absolute, or what amounts to a fee simple absolute, will convey a fee simple absolute under the modern trend. Any words of limitation that do not expressly limit the estate what is being conveyed will be presumed to convey a fee simple absolute.

---

the grant (the initial cross line) to eternity (the end of the time line). If O conveys a possessory estate short of a fee simple absolute, there must be at least one future interest. In diagramming property interests, each estate which is less than a fee simple absolute must have a cross line to the *right* of the initial conveyance cross line to indicate the end of the estate and the beginning of the future interest following the estate. And at least one of the future interests must be of fee simple absolute duration to account for the whole time line. These diagramming guidelines will make more sense as the material diagrams the basic possessory estate and future interest combinations.

[25] PROPERTY RESTATEMENT, *supra* note 10, at §§ 39-41. For further discussion of the difference between the common law approach and the modern trend approach to the necessary words of limitation to create the different estates, *see* discussion *infra* Ch. 4, II, A.

The following examples demonstrate the difference between the common law and modern trend approach to the words of limitation necessary to convey a fee simple absolute:

EXAMPLE 3

O → To A forever.

O → To A.

O → To A and her heirs.

Under the common law approach, only the last conveyance would transfer a fee simple absolute. Under the modern trend approach, all three conveyances would transfer a fee simple absolute. The grantor's intent arguably is clearer under the common law approach, but the modern trend implicitly acknowledges that not all drafters/grantors know or use proper terminology. The modern trend arguably focuses more on intent, but at a higher cost of administration; the common law approach takes more of a bright line/low cost of administration approach which may, on occasion, frustrate a grantor's intent. The material will generally use, and expect you to use, the common law approach. Your professor, however, may use the modern trend approach, so you should be familiar with both.

IV. TRANSFERABILITY, DEVISABILITY, INHERITABILITY

There are basically three ways to convey a property interest. A property interest is **transferable** if, while the owner of the interest is alive, he or she can freely transfer it to any third party. A property interest is **devisable** if, upon the owner's death, he or she can freely will it in his or her last will and testament to any third party. And a property interest is **inheritable** if the heirs of the owner of the interest can inherit the property interest if the owner dies without a valid will.[26] The fee simple absolute is freely transferable, devisable and inheritable.[27]

---

[26] Or with a valid will, if the will does not dispose of the property interest in question.

[27] MOYNIHAN, *supra* note 9, at 26.

THE DIFFERENT CATEGORIES OF POSSESSORY ESTATES
AND THEIR FUTURE INTERESTS

CATEGORY	POSSESSORY ESTATE(S) (words of limitation)	FUTURE INTERESTS	
		GRANTOR PARTY	THIRD
FEE SIMPLE ABSOLUTE	FEE SIMPLE ABSOLUTE (and her heirs)	NONE	NONE

PROBLEM SET 1

Which of the following conveyances properly transfers a fee simple absolute to the grantee under: (a) the common law rules of drafting; and (b) the modern trend rules of drafting? (*The answers to all of the problems in the book are set forth in the back of the book in Appendix A.*)

1.   O →   To A and his children.

     (a) Common law:

     (b) Modern trend:

2.   O →   To A and his heirs.

     (a) Common law:

     (b) Modern trend:

3.   O →   To A in fee simple absolute.

     (a) Common law:

     (b) Modern trend:

4.   O →   To the heirs of A.

   (a) Common law:

   (b) Modern trend:

5.   O →   To B.

   (a) Common law:

   (b) Modern trend:

6.   O →   All to A.

   (a) Common law:

   (b) Modern trend:

7.   O →   To A forever.

   (a) Common law:

   (b) Modern trend:

Chapter 3

FEE SIMPLE DEFEASIBLES

I. OVERVIEW

The second category of possessory estates is the **fee simple defeasibles**. While the defining characteristic of the fee simple absolute is that in theory it will last forever, the defining characteristic of the fee simple defeasibles is that they **may** last forever.

II. THE FEE SIMPLE DEFEASIBLES

A. NATURE OF THE ESTATE

A classic example of a fee simple defeasible is as follows:

EXAMPLE 1

O → to A and her heirs, but if A sells alcohol on the land, then O has the right to re-enter and reclaim the land.

Notice the wording of the conveyance begins just like that for a fee simple absolute. The first two words, "To A ..." again are the words of purchase which indicate to whom the property interest is being conveyed. The words immediately following the words of purchase typically are the words of limitation which will help indicate which possessory estate is being conveyed. Here, the phrase immediately following the words of purchase is "and her heirs" – the classic words of limitation for the fee simple absolute. But in example 1 above, the wording of the conveyance goes on to indicate that the fee simple being conveyed is not absolute but rather is qualified by a restriction or condition – "as long as A does not sell alcohol on the land." If A were to sell alcohol on the land, A would lose the right to possess the property. A's right to possession is not absolute but is defeasible (subject to being terminated) if the express condition were to occur.

The additional language qualifying what would otherwise be a fee simple absolute is what distinguishes the fee simple defeasibles from the other possessory estates. The uncertain nature of the condition or restriction (whether it will occur or not) is such that the possessory estate may last forever (if the condition or restriction never occurs), but the possessory estate **may end** (if the condition or restriction occurs).[28]

So if the language of the conveyance starts out like a fee simple absolute, but then there is an express condition subsequent after the fee simple words of limitation qualifying the fee simple, the possessory estate is one of the fee simple defeasibles. There are three fee simple defeasibles: (1) the **fee simple determinable**; (2) the **fee simple subject to a condition subsequent**, and (3) the **fee simple subject to an executory limitation**.

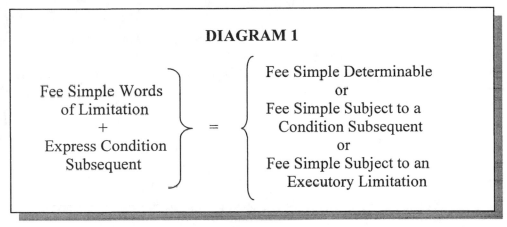

DIAGRAM 1

Fee Simple Words of Limitation + Express Condition Subsequent } = { Fee Simple Determinable or Fee Simple Subject to a Condition Subsequent or Fee Simple Subject to an Executory Limitation

Inasmuch as there are three different fee simple defeasibles, the next step analytically is to know how to distinguish among the three.

B. ANALYZING THE FEE SIMPLE DEFEASIBLES

The characteristics that distinguish one fee simple defeasible from another are: (1) who holds the future interest – the original grantor or a third party (anyone other than the grantor); and (2) if the grantor retains the

---

[28] Notice that the qualifying condition is a condition **subsequent** – temporally it applies to the party's right to keep possession **after** the party takes actual possession. The express qualifying condition in Example 1, "as long as A does not sell alcohol on the land," implicitly assumes that A has taken **actual** possession. A cannot sell alcohol on the land if A does not have the right to actual possession of the land. The material will not focus on this point here, but later it will become important and the material will address it in greater detail. It might help to keep this in mind as you move through this chapter.

future interest, how does the condition subsequent, if it occurs, cut short the fee simple – automatically or only upon the grantor's actions.

1. Ask "Who Holds the Future Interest?"

The first step in distinguishing the fee simple defeasibles from each other is to ask "**who holds the future interest**." If the future interest[29] is held by the grantor, the fee simple defeasible can be one of only two possibilities: a fee simple determinable or a fee simple subject to a condition subsequent. On the other hand, if the future interest is held by a third party, there is only one possibility: a fee simple subject to an executory limitation:

DIAGRAM 2

FSD +

FI in Grantor   =   Fee Simple Determinable
or
Fee Simple Subject to Condition Subsequent

FI in Third Party   =   Fee Simple Subject to an Executory Limitation

---

2. Grantor Holds Future Interest: Fee Simple Determinable vs. Fee Simple Subject to a Condition Subsequent

Where the possessory estate is a fee simple defeasible, and the future interest is held by the grantor, the fee simple defeasible is either: (1) a **fee simple determinable**; or (2) a **fee simple subject to a condition subsequent**. These are the only two possibilities.

---

[29] A future interest again is the right to possession after the possessory estate ends, here, after the fee simple defeasible.

DIAGRAM 3

Fee Simple Defeasible + FI in Grantor = $\left\{\begin{array}{c} \text{Fee Simple Determinable} \\ \text{or} \\ \text{Fee Simple Subject to a} \\ \text{Condition Subsequent} \end{array}\right.$

The key to distinguishing these two fee simple defeasibles turns on **how** the condition subsequent, if it occurs, cuts short the fee simple: automatically or upon the grantor's actions. If the grantor's intent is to terminate the fee simple *automatically* the moment the express qualifying condition occurs, the possessory estate is a **fee simple determinable**. On the other hand, if the grantor's intent is *not* to terminate the possessory estate automatically the moment the qualifying condition occurs, but rather to give the grantor the **right of entry**[30] to reclaim the property (also known as the **power of termination**[31]), the possessory estate is a **fee simple subject to a condition subsequent**.

While this conceptual difference may seem trivial,[32] you need to be able to distinguish these two possessory estates. Moreover, although in theory the key is the grantor's intent, the traditional common law approach focused more on the express language used in the conveyance. The traditional

---

[30] Technically, under the common law approach, it is also known as a "right of entry for breach of condition/for condition broken" clause. MOYNIHAN, *supra* note 9, at 112.

[31] The modern trend prefers to call the future interest a power to terminate. This stems from the modern trend aversion to self-help. The common law right of re-entry literally required the grantor to re-enter the land to terminate the fee simple. The problem was that the party holding the possessory estate may resist the grantor's attempt at re-entry. The potential for violence, both to the parties and to innocent by-standers, has led the modern trend to repudiate self-help and to require the party (here the grantor) to use the court system to exercise his or her rights. Hence the preference under the modern trend to call the future interest following a fee simple subject to a condition subsequent a "power to terminate" rather than a "right of entry."

[32] The conceptual difference in how the fee simple determinable ends affects when the statute of limitations for adverse possession begins. Assuming the express condition occurs and the party who held the possessory estate does not vacate the land, with the fee simple determinable the statute of limitations begins to run immediately upon the condition occurring, whether the party who held the future interest (the grantor) knows or not that the condition has occurred. On the other hand, with the fee simple subject to a condition subsequent, the condition's occurrence only gives the grantor the right to re-enter and retake the property, it does not start the statute of limitations for adverse possession until the grantor tries to re-enter the property and is denied entry.

common law approach created a virtual irrebuttable presumption that certain words of limitation evidenced a certain grantor's intent. Accordingly, the key to distinguishing the two fee simple defeasibles where the future interest is held by the grantor is the words of limitation used to introduce the qualifying condition.

The classic words of limitation evidencing a fee simple determinable – the intent that the possessory estate terminate automatically the moment the qualifying condition occurs – is the phrase: "to A and her heirs **as long as/so long as** ... ." Other words used less commonly but equally effective are "**until** ...", "**during** ...", and "**while** ... ."[33] In contrast, the classic words of limitation evidencing a fee simple subject to a condition subsequent – the intent that the possessory estate *not* terminate automatically the moment the qualifying condition occurs, but rather continues until the grantor re-enters and re-claims the property – is the phrase "to A and her heirs, **but if** ...". Other words used less commonly but equally effective are "**however, if** ..." and "**provided that** ... ."[34] In addition, where the fee simple subject to a condition subsequent words of limitation are present, they should be coupled with a clause (after the clause expressing the qualifying condition) which expressly states that O has the right to re-enter and re-take the property in the event the condition occurs.[35]

EXAMPLE 2

O →   To A and her heirs, but if A sells alcohol on the land, then O has the right to re-enter and reclaim the land.

The express clause in the conveyance giving O the right to re-enter and retake the land is known as a "**right of entry clause**." The presence of a right of entry clause in favor of the grantor makes it much easier to identify the fee simple subject to a condition subsequent. If the express right of entry clause is not present, its absence typically creates ambiguity over which fee simple defeasible the grantor intended. Recourse to the introductory words of limitation before the qualifying condition becomes the next best evidence of which fee simple defeasible the grantor intended.

---

[33] PROPERTY RESTATEMENT, *supra* note 10, at § 44, cmt. l.
[34] PROPERTY RESTATEMENT, *supra* note 10, at § 45, cmt. j.
[35] *Id.*

Where the language is ambiguous, the courts tend to favor a fee simple subject to a condition subsequent because of the judicial disfavor for forfeiture.[36]

Just as with the fee simple absolute, the fee simple defeasibles can be diagramed on a time line:

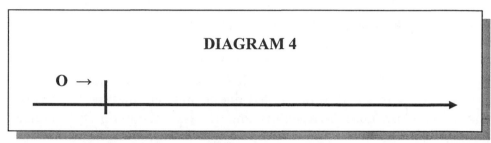

The whole, uninterrupted arrow to the right of the initial conveyance cross line would constitute a fee simple absolute. Inasmuch as the distinguishing feature of the fee simple defeasible estates is that they **may** end at some point in the future, this possibility is indicated by a **dashed** cross line at some point on the arrow (to the right of the point in time when the fee simple defeasible estate was created):

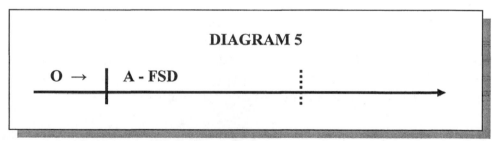

Diagram 5 reflects that the fee simple *may* end (hence the dotted line, as opposed to solid line), if the qualifying condition occurs. Diagram 5 depicts the fee simple determinable/fee simple subject to an executory limitation.[37]

---

[36] Notice that if the conveyance is construed as a fee simple determinable and the condition occurs, the effect is immediate and automatic **forfeiture** of the possessory estate; with the fee simple subject to a condition subsequent, if the condition occurs the possessory estate does not end until the grantor asserts his or her right of entry. Because of judicial disfavor for forfeiture, many courts prefer to construe ambiguous conveyances as fee simple subject to a condition subsequent. MOYNIHAN, *supra* note 9, at 109.

[37] Regardless of whether fee simple determinable or fee simple subject to a condition subsequent language is used to introduce the qualifying condition, where the future interest is given to a third party, the courts have ruled that the fee simple subject to an executory limitation terminates automatically upon the occurrence of the express condition subsequent.

If the qualifying condition occurs, the fee simple will end automatically the moment the condition subsequent occurs. But if the qualifying condition does not occur, the fee simple will last forever.

The diagram for the fee simple subject to a condition subsequent needs to be modified slightly to reflect that under it, if the qualifying condition occurs, the estate does not end immediately and automatically. The estate does not end unless, and until, O exercises **the right of entry/power of termination**. Graphically, the easiest way to indicate this distinguishing feature of the fee simple subject to a condition subsequent is to again use a dashed cross line (to indicate that the estate **may** end), only this time an arrow is added to the dotted line to indicate that the estate does not end unless and until O re-enters and re-takes the property/exercises the power to terminate:

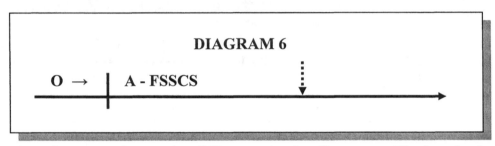

DIAGRAM 6

O → | A - FSSCS

The key, however, is not the difference in the diagrams. The key is the conceptual difference between the fee simple determinable and the fee simple subject to a condition subsequent which leads to the difference in their words of limitation and classifying terminology.

3.   Future interest in Third Party – The Fee Simple Subject to an Executory Limitation

If the future interest following a fee simple defeasible is held by **a third party**, the fee simple defeasible must be a **fee simple subject to an executory limitation**.[38] And there is one, and only one, future interest which goes with fee simple subject to an executory limitation – an **executory interest**.[39]

LEWIS M. SIMES & ALLAN F. SMITH, THE LAW OF FUTURE INTERESTS 266 (2nd ed., West 1956); Bean v. Atkins, 89 A.2d 643 (Va. 1914).

[38] PROPERTY RESTATEMENT, *supra* note 10, at § 46, cmt. e.

[39] One can argue that there are *two* possible future interests which can follow a fee simple subject to an executory limitation because the executory interest can be either a

---

EXAMPLE 3

O → To A and her heirs, but if A sells alcohol on the land,
then to B and her heirs.

In analyzing the conveyance in Example 3,[40] the first question is which category of estates does the possessory estate belong in – fee simple absolute or fee simple defeasibles? Although the first five words of the conveyance are the classic words of purchase and words of limitation for a fee simple absolute, the conveyance goes on to impose an express restriction on how long A's possessory estate may last (an express condition subsequent). The fee simple may end if A sells alcohol on the land. The possessory estate is a fee simple defeasible.

To determine which fee simple defeasible it is, the first step is to ask "who takes" the future interest following the fee simple defeasible – the grantor or a third party. Here B, a third party holds the future interest. Because a party other than the grantor holds the future interest, the possessory estate is a fee simple subject to an executory limitation and the future interest is an executory interest.

C. ANALYZING FUTURE INTERESTS WHICH FOLLOW A FEE SIMPLE DEFEASIBLE

The estates described so far, the fee simple determinable, the fee simple subject to a condition subsequent, and the fee simple subject to an executory limitation, describe the **possessory** estates in the second category of estates: the **fee simple defeasibles**. Inasmuch as there is the

---

shifting or a springing executory interest. *See* discussion *infra* Ch. 3, II, C, 4.

[40] Notice the analytical steps performed in analyzing the conveyance. First, determine who takes the possessory estate and in which category of possessory estates it falls. Once you determine which category it is, determine which possessory estate within that category it is (for the fee simple defeasibles, that requires you to ask "who takes" the future interest). Then, if the possessory estate is not a fee simple absolute, analyze the future interest(s). In analyzing each future interest, remember that there are three steps: (1) identify who holds the future interest; (2) identify which future interest it is, and (3) determine which possessory estate the future interest will be if and when it becomes possessory. This is the basic analytical scheme that should be performed over and over for each conveyance.

possibility that each of these possessory estates **may** end, there **must** be a future interest which follows each of these possessory estates. **Each possessory estate other than a fee simple absolute must be coupled with a future interest**. Again, a future interest is the **present** right to possess the property **in the future**. At the time the fee simple defeasible is created, because the grantor did not transfer a fee simple absolute to the party holding the possessory interest, by definition there must be a future interest. Someone must have the **present** right (at the time the possessory interest is created) to possess the property the moment the possessory estate terminates at some point in the future.

There are three steps to analyzing each future interest:[41] (1) identify **who holds** the future interest; (2) state **the name of the future interest**; and (3) state **the duration of the future interest**.

1. Step One: Identify Who Holds The Future Interest?

Just as with the possessory estate, the first step in analyzing future interests is to identify to whom the interest was granted. The easiest way to identify the holder of the future interest is to examine the express language of the conveyance to see who will receive the property if the qualifying condition occurs. For example:

EXAMPLE 4

O →   To A and her heirs, but if A sells alcohol on the land,
         then O has the right to re-enter and reclaim the land.

Although it looks like A has a fee simple absolute from the phrase "to A and her heirs," the additional qualifying language indicates that A must hold a fee simple defeasible. Which fee simple defeasible turns on who holds the future interest. In Example 4, the future interest is retained by O, the grantor, so the possessory estate must be either a fee simple determinable or a fee simple subject to a condition subsequent. Analyzing further, the words of limitation "but if ..." indicate a fee simple subject to a condition subsequent. The next

---

[41] Obviously the remainder of this discussion assumes there is a future interest. If the possessory estate is a fee simple absolute, there is no future interest. For all other possessory estates, however, there must be a future interest.

clause **(reading comma to comma)** indicates to whom the right to possession passes in the event the condition occurs. Here, the express language indicates that O holds the future interest.

The easiest way to determine *who holds* the future interest is to look for the **express** words of purchase in the clause introducing the future interest. That statement assumes, however, that there are express words of purchase. For each possessory estate, there **must** be express words of purchase or there is no conveyance. But unlike possessory estates, future interests can be created by default. A future interest can arise by default where the grantor creates a possessory estate which is **not** a fee simple absolute, but the conveyance does *not* indicate expressly to whom the future interest is granted. Someone must have the right to possession in the event the fee simple is cut short – so there must be a future interest. The common law courts reasoned that if the conveyance did not expressly indicate to whom the future interest was conveyed, the grantor must have intended to retain the interest. Thus, **if there is no express language indicating to whom the future interest is granted, by default the courts imply that the future interest is retained/held by the grantor in fee simple**.

For example, what if the conveyance read as follows:

EXAMPLE 5

O →   To A and her heirs as long as she does not sell liquor on the land.

The express words of the conveyance indicate that the grantor intended to create a fee simple defeasible, but the conveyance does not indicate who holds the future interest. [42] Because the possessory estate in Example 5 is a fee

---

[42] If the material is using proper drafting techniques, why not just make the future interest express?

     O →   To A and her heirs as long as she does not sell liquor on the land,
           then to O and her heirs.

At common law, the grantor could **not expressly** create a future interest in the grantor following a fee simple determinable. Although the rule has been abolished today in many jurisdictions, the common law courts ruled that a grantor could not expressly *grant* an interest to him or herself, but he or she could retain an interest. The rationale for the rule lies in the livery of seisin ceremony, which is beyond the scope of this material. But the effect of the

simple defeasible, there *must be* a future interest (because the duration of the last express estate is a fee simple defeasible – which is less than a fee simple absolute).   But the conveyance does not expressly state who holds it.   By default the grantor must hold the future interest.   Because the future interest is held by the grantor, and the possessory estate is a fee simple defeasible, the possessory estate must be a fee simple determinable or a fee simple subject to a condition subsequent.   The words of limitation introducing the qualifying condition are "as long as," so the possessory estate is a fee simple determinable.

2. Step Two: Identify Which Future Interest It Is

After identifying who holds the future interest, the second step in analyzing each future interest is to identify (by proper name) which future interest the party holds.   The name of the future interest turns primarily on: (1) **which possessory estate it follows**,[43] and (2) **who holds** the future interest.

Each possessory estate can be coupled with only a limited number of possible future interests.[44]   For purposes of this introductory coverage, there is only one future interest which can follow each fee simple defeasible.   The **only future interest which can follow a fee simple determinable is a possibility of reverter**.[45]   These two estates, the fee simple determinable and the possibility of reverter, go hand in hand and should not be coupled with any other estates.   The **only future interest which can follow a fee simple subject to a condition subsequent is a right of entry/power of termination**.[46]   These two estates go hand in hand.   The **only future interest**

---

common law rule is that you need to pay close attention to the default rule – if the grantor holds a fee simple absolute and does not convey the whole fee simple absolute, the grantor is the default holder of the future interest, because at early common law that was the only way a grantor could create a possibility of reverter (or, as you will see, a reversion) in him or herself.

[43] For some future interests, *how it terminates* the possessory estate is also a factor.

[44] This is particularly true for an introductory coverage.   A more extensive coverage of possessory estates and future interests would introduce many more possible combinations. But that is beyond the scope of this material.

[45] PROPERTY RESTATEMENT, *supra* note 10, at § 154, cmt. g.   And conversely, in this introductory coverage the possibility of reverter follows one, and only one, estate: a fee simple determinable.   *But see* discussion *infra* Ch. 9, where the material raises the possibility of defeasible finite estates.

[46] PROPERTY RESTATEMENT, *supra* note 10, at § 155, cmt. b.   And conversely, in this introductory coverage, the right of entry/power of termination follows one, and only one,

which can follow a fee simple subject to an executory limitation is an
executory interest.[47] These two estates go hand in hand. Although the
names of the future interests help somewhat in remembering which future
interest goes with which possessory estate,[48] this is where rote memorization
becomes important.

3. Step Three: Indicate the Duration of the Future Interest

After (1) identifying **who holds** the future interest, and (2) stating the
name of the future interest, the final step in analyzing each future interest is to
indicate the **duration** of the future interest. The *name* of a future interest
indicates only that the interest is a future interest – that the party who holds
the interest has the right to claim actual possession of the property at some
point in the future. The name of the future interest does *not* indicate how long
the party has the right to actual possession once the interest becomes
possessory. How long will the right to actual possession last? The analysis
with respect to the duration of a future interest is basically the same as the
analysis of the duration of a possessory estate. Examine the express clause
granting the future interest and look for the words of limitation which indicate
the duration of the interest if and when it becomes possessory.[49] Where the
future interest arises by default (i.e., there is no clause expressly granting the
future interest to a party), the default taker is the grantor. The duration of a
default future interest is in fee simple as a general rule.[50]

---

estate: a fee simple subject to a condition subsequent. (*But see* discussion *infra* Ch. 9, where
the material raises the possibility of defeasible finite estates.)

[47] PROPERTY RESTATEMENT, *supra* note 10, at § 158.

[48] Notice how the different terms for the future interests reflect the conceptual
difference between the two possessory estates. With the fee simple determinable, if the condition
occurs, the possessory estate automatically ends and the property automatically reverts to the
grantor; hence the term **possibility of reverter.** With the fee simple subject to a condition
subsequent, if the express condition occurs, the grantor has a **right of entry** to reclaim the property;
hence the term **right** of entry. Remembering the conceptual difference between the two fee simple
defeasible estates can help you remember the correct coupling of the possessory estates and future
interests.

[49] If the future interest is in fee simple absolute, then that usually is the end of the
analysis. On the other hand, if the future interest is some estate less than a fee simple absolute,
then that future interest must be followed by yet another future interest until a future interest of fee
simple absolute duration is identified.

[50] That statement assumes, as is the norm, that the default future interest is an
unqualified default future interest. The material will introduce more complex conveyances
later where one could argue that there is a qualified default future interest, and because the
qualification is express, the duration is not a fee simple absolute but rather a fee simple
subject to an executory limitation. But do not worry about that exception to the general rule

As applied to the fee simple defeasibles, because of the limited combinations of estates covered in the introductory treatment, the three step analysis of each future interest[51] is greatly simplified because of a number of sub-rules which emerge. First, there is one, and only one, future interest which goes with each fee simple defeasible.   Once you determine the possessory estate is a *fee simple determinable, the future interest must be a possibility of reverter*; once you determine the possessory estate is a *fee simple subject to a condition subsequent, the future interest must be a right of entry/power of termination*; once you determine that the possessory estate is a fee simple subject to an executory limitation, the future interest *must be an executory interest*. Second, whichever future interest it is, the duration of the future interest will always be in fee simple absolute. This greatly facilitates analysis of the fee simple defeasibles.   Once you determine that the possessory estate is a fee simple determinable, the future interest *must be a possibility of reverter in fee simple absolute*. Once you determine that the possessory estate is a fee simple subject to a condition subsequent, the future interest *must be a right of entry/power of termination in fee simple absolute*. Once you determine that the possessory estate is a fee simple subject to an executory limitation, the future interest *must be an executory interest in fee simple absolute.*[52]

4. If Future Interest is Executory Interest – Step 4: Shifting vs. Springing Executory Interests

Where the future interest is an executory interest, there is one further analytical step that must be performed: you must indicate **which type** of executory interest it is. There are two types of executory interests: **shifting** executory interests and **springing** executory interests. In analyzing which type it is, focus on who held the legal right to possession under the estate

---

until later.

[51] First, who holds the future interest (focus on the express words of purchase – "to whom?"); second, what is the name of the future interest (focus on what estate does the future interest follow), and third, what is the duration of the future interest (focus on the express words of limitation in the clause creating the future interest).

[52] At about this point in the material students begin to realize that rote memorization of the different terms is an integral part of the analytical steps. If you do not know the steps in the analysis, it is difficult (if not impossible) to analyze the possessory estates and future interests created by a conveyance. But if you do not know the terminology, it is difficult (if not impossible) to analyze the possessory estates and future interests created by a conveyance. You must focus on both the terminology and the steps in the analysis.

immediately preceding the executory interest; analytically ask "from whom is the right to possession being taken." An executory interest is a **shifting** executory interest if the right to possession under the future interest is being taken from a third party (i.e., someone other than the grantor).[53] The executory interest is a **springing executory interest** if the right to possession is being taken from the grantor.[54] While this analysis sounds very abstract, it is very easy in application.

Return to Example 3:

EXAMPLE 3

O → To A and her heirs, but if A sells alcohol on the land, then to B and her heirs.

A holds a fee simple subject to an executory limitation, and B holds an executory interest. Is B's interest a shifting or a springing executory interest? From whom is the party holding the future interest taking the right to possession – the grantor or a third party? Here, B is taking the right to possession from A, a third party. B holds a shifting executory interest.

The third step in analyzing future interests is to state the duration of the future interest. If and when the future interest becomes possessory, how long will the party have the right to keep actual possession? Analytically this is the same as asking, which possessory estate does B hold? The duration of an estate is almost always determined by the express words of limitation relative to that party's estate. Find the words of purchase with respect to that party, and then find the words of limitation (which typically immediately follow the words of purchase) that indicate the duration of the future estate if and when it becomes possessory. Here the final clause provides "then to B and her heirs." The words of purchase indicate that B holds the future interest (which we have already determined above is a

---

[53] PROPERTY RESTATEMENT, *supra* note 10, at § 46, cmt. k.

[54] PROPERTY RESTATEMENT, *supra* note 10, at § 46, cmt. l. Springing executory interests are the rarer of the two executory interests. The material will examine springing executory interests in greater detail when covering the more unusual conveyances where they tend to arise. *See* discussion *infra* Ch. 7, II.

shifting executory interest).   The words of limitation *"and her heirs"* indicate that the duration of the future interest is a fee simple absolute.[55]

Putting it all together, the full state of the title in Example 3 is: A holds a fee simple subject to an executory limitation, and B holds a shifting executory interest in fee simple.

III. TRANSFERABILITY, DEVISEABILITY, INHERITABILITY

The fee simple defeasibles (the fee simple determinable, the fee simple subject to a condition subsequent, and the fee simple subject to an executory interest) are freely transferable, inheritable and devisable – subject to the express condition in the conveyance. The future interests following a fee simple defeasible, however, are not as freely transferable, devisable, and inheritable. The common law rule was that a possibility of reverter and a right of entry/power of termination could be held only by the grantor. Consistent with this general rule, the common law courts ruled that the possibility of reverter and the right of entry/power of termination were not transferable or devisable, only inheritable by the grantor's heirs – thereby keeping the future interest in the grantor's bloodline.[56] Because of the uncertain nature of executory interests (they may become possessory, they may not), the common law courts reasoned that they were not transferable, but they were inheritable and devisable.[57]

---

[55] Although there are a myriad of different possible combinations of possessory estates and future interests, certain generalizations apply to the introductory coverage of possessory estates and future interests. First, for each of the fee simple defeasibles, there is one and only one future interest which will follow it. Second, if the possessory estate is a fee simple subject to an executory limitation, the future interest will always be an executory interest – and it will always be in fee simple. The only other analytical step you will need to perform is to determine whether the executory interest is a shifting or springing executory interest. That will turn on from whom the future interest is taking the right to possession – a third party (a shifting executory interest) or the grantor (a springing executory interest).

[56] Mahrenholz v. County Board of School Trustees, 417 N.E.2d 138 (Ill. App. Ct. 1981).

[57] RICHARD R. POWELL, POWELL ON REAL PROPERTY ¶ 283, at 252 (Patrick J. Rohan ed., 1979).

Under the modern trend, the general rule is that the possibility of reverter and executory interests are freely transferable, inheritable, and devisable.[58] But as a general rule, the right of entry/power of termination is still not transferable, though it is inheritable and devisable.[59]

---

[58] MOYNIHAN, *supra* note 9, at 110-111, 199.
[59] *Id.* at 115-117.

RECAP

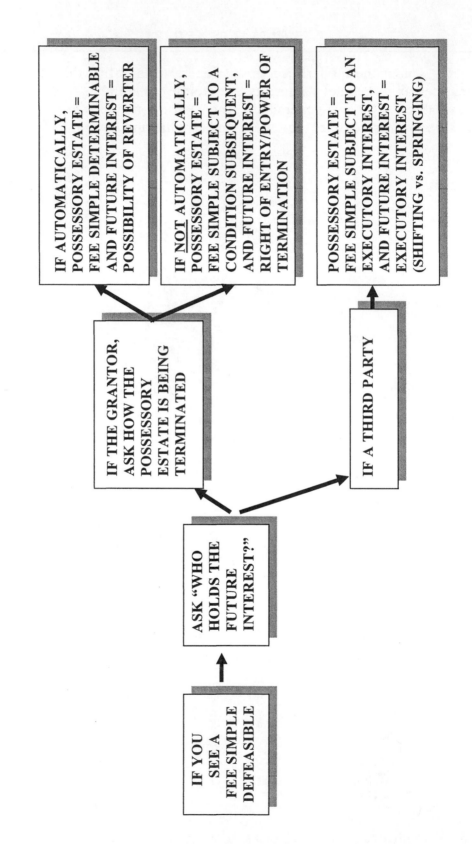

CATEGORY OF POSSESSORY ESTATES	POSSESSORY ESTATE(S) (words of limitation)	FUTURE INTERESTS	
		GRANTOR	THIRD PARTY
FEE SIMPLE ABSOLUTE	FEE SIMPLE ABSOLUTE (and her heirs)	NONE	NONE
FEE SIMPLE DEFEASIBLES	FEE SIMPLE DETERMINABLE (and her heirs as long as/while/until)	POSSIBILITY OF REVERTER	NONE
	FEE SIMPLE SUBJECT TO A CONDITION SUBSEQUENT (and her heirs, but if … right to enter)	RIGHT OF ENTRY/ POWER OF TERMINATION	NONE
	FEE SIMPLE SUBJECT TO AN EXECUTORY LIMITATION (and her heirs as long as/but if)	NONE	EXECUTORY LIMITATION (shifting vs. springing)

PROBLEM SET 2

State the title for the following conveyances. It might also help if you diagramed the conveyances (but if not, do not force yourself; some students find this helpful, others do not).

1.   O →   To A and her heirs as long as she uses the land for educational purposes.

2.   O →   To A and her heirs, but if she stops using the land for educational purposes, then O has the right to re-enter and re-claim the land.

3.   O →   To A and her heirs as long as she does not re-marry, then to B and his heirs.

4.   O →   To A and her heirs, but if A remarries, then to B and his heirs.

O →

5.   O →   To A and her heirs if she graduates from law school.

Chapter 4

THE FINITE ESTATES

I. OVERVIEW

The third category of possessory estates is the finite estates. While the first category, fee simple absolute, in theory, *will* last forever, and while the second category, the fee simple defeasibles, *may* last forever, the defining characteristic of the third category of estates is that they *must end.* The three finite estates are the **life estate,** the **fee tail,** and the **term of years.** Because they **must end,** the third category of estates may be referred to collectively as the **finite estates.**[60]

II. THE FINITE ESTATES

The distinguishing characteristic of the finite estates, that they *must* end, is reflected in the terminology. Unlike the first two categories of estates (the fee simple absolute and the fee simple defeasibles), **none** of the three finite possessory estates includes the phrase "fee simple" in its name. Moreover, the finite nature of the life estate, the fee tail and the term of years is also reflected in their respective words of limitation. As you will see, **none** of the three includes the phrase "and her heirs/and his heirs" in its words of limitation.

Having identified the common characteristic which distinguishes the life estate, the fee tail and term of years from the other possessory estates (that the estate **must** end), the question becomes what distinguishes these three estates from each other. The distinguishing trait, as one might expect, is in their **duration.** Although all of the final three possessory estates are finite, they are of different finite durations.

---

[60] To distinguish them from the fee simple defeasible estates, which may end, and the fee simple absolute, which in theory never ends.

A. THE LIFE ESTATE

As its name indicates, the distinguishing characteristic of the **life estate** is that it lasts for the duration of the **grantee's** life.[61]   A classic example of a life estate is the following:

EXAMPLE 1

O → To A for life.

The words of limitation which indicate a life estate is the simple phrase "for life."

At common law, however, the life estate was also the **default estate.** The default estate is the estate which results if the grantor fails to draft properly one of the other possessory estates. Accordingly, in the following example:

EXAMPLE 2

O → To A.

There are no express words of limitation indicating the duration of A's possessory estate. At common law, because the life estate was the default estate, A would be deemed to have a life estate. Moreover, even if the conveyance were as follows:

EXAMPLE 3

O → To A in fee simple absolute.

A would only hold a life estate at common law. To create a fee simple absolute at common law, the grantor had to use the proper words of

---

[61] PROPERTY RESTATEMENT, *supra* note 10, at § 18.

limitation – "and her heirs." Common law was very demanding in requiring use of the appropriate words of limitation.

The modern trend presumes that the grantor intends to convey all that he or she has in the absence of express words of limitation indicating the intent to limit the estate being conveyed. Thus, under the modern trend, the default estate is the fee simple absolute (assuming that is what the grantor held).[62] Accordingly, the above examples (8 and 9) would both convey a fee simple absolute if that is what O owned at the time of the conveyance. For drafting purposes, however, you should not depend upon a rule of construction to resolve any ambiguity inherent in a conveyance. The appropriate words of limitation should be used.[63]

A grantee may transfer his or her life estate inter vivos. If a life tenant transfers his or her interest, the grantee/transferee holds a life estate *pur autre vie*: a life estate measured by the life of another (i.e., measured by the life of the original life tenant). For example, if a party holding a life estate (say "A") transfers his or her life estate to another ("B"), because one cannot transfer more than one owns, the grantee/transferee (B) would hold a life estate measured by the original life tenant's life (A's life – or a life estate *pur autre vie*). While A is still alive, B's life estate *pur autre vie* is transferable, inheritable and devisable,[64] but upon A's death the life estate *pur autre vie* immediately expires - even if B is still alive.

B. THE FEE TAIL

The second finite estate is the fee tail. In theory, a fee tail is a series of life estates. At common law, a fee tail was a life estate to the immediate grantee, and upon his or her death, a life estate to his or her children, and upon each child's death, a life estate to that child's children, and so on until there were no "children" to take the fee tail.[65] The words of

---

[62] PROPERTY RESTATEMENT, *supra* note 10, at §§ 39-41.

[63] You should use proper drafting terminology, and thus the material will use proper drafting terminology and the common law rule of construction unless otherwise indicated. But if proper drafting language is not used, you need to pay careful attention to whether the common law or modem trend rules of construction/default rules apply.

[64] If B dies, but A, the original life tenant is still alive, B's life estate *pur autre vie* would go into B's probate estate, where B could devise it if he or she had a valid will; otherwise it would pass through intestacy to B's heirs.

[65] PROPERTY RESTATEMENT, *supra* note 10, at § 59.

limitation necessary to create a fee tail are "**and the heirs of his/her body**." For example:

EXAMPLE 4

O → To A and the heirs of her body, then to B and the heirs of his body.

The phrase "and the heirs of her body" indicates the series of life estates, one generation after another, limited to the heirs of the body (the lineal descendants) of the identified grantee.

In essence, the fee tail is a series of life estates in a family blood line. Conceptually, this can be a bit mind boggling. On the one hand, it is conceivable that the bloodline could continue for eternity, in which case it looks something like a fee simple defeasible (possibly the reason why it is called a fee tail). On the other hand, it is also conceivable that there could be no child to take the fee tail interest and it could end upon the death of the immediate grantee (i.e., it would last as a practical matter no longer than a single life estate). For purposes of analysis, the latter is the better way to think about the fee tail. Common law assumed that sooner or later the family line would die out, and, therefore, the analysis and future interest terminology for the fee tail are the same as for the life estate.

One additional twist to the fee tail is that the grantor can limit the eligible heirs of the body of the immediate grantee. The grantor can limit the fee tail to the male heirs of the grantee by drafting a **fee tail male**:[66]

EXAMPLE 5

O → To A and the male heirs of her body.

The grantor can limit the fee tail to the female heirs of the grantee by drafting a **fee tail female**:[67]

---

[66] PROPERTY RESTATEMENT, *supra* note 10, at § 59, cmt. e.

EXAMPLE 6

O → To A and the female heirs of her body.

The grantor could limit the fee tail to any characteristic he or she wished. Nevertheless, such conveyances were still fee tails with the operative words of limitation "and the heirs of her body."

C.   THE TERM OF YEARS

The final finite possessory estate is the **term of years**.   The defining characteristic of a term of years estate is that the express language of the conveyance establishes a **finite duration which is calculable on the day the interest is created**[68] **– the end date must be capable of being determined on the first day the interest becomes possessory**. Despite its name, term of **years,** the estate need not be a year or longer.   The only requirement is that the exact term of the estate must be calculable on the first day of the term.   Although there is a plethora of different ways to express a finite time period, a couple of classic examples of term of years estates are as follows:

EXAMPLE 7

O → To A for 5 years.

O → To A from January 1, 2006 until December 31, 2010.

The classic words of limitation indicating a term of years possessory estate are the phrases "for (some finite time period)" or "from (a date certain) to (another date certain)."

---

[67] *Id.*

[68] PROPERTY RESTATEMENT, *supra* note 10, at § 19, cmt. b.

III. FUTURE INTERESTS FOLLOWING A FINITE ESTATE

Inasmuch as the defining characteristic of the finite estates (the life estate, the fee tail, and the term of years) is that they **must** end, there **must** be a future interest following each. This point can be demonstrated by diagramming the finite estates on the time line. Because each of the finite estates **must** end, each can be diagramed as a relatively short segment of the arrow with a solid cross line at the right end of the line segment indicating the estate **must end** at some point short of infinity:

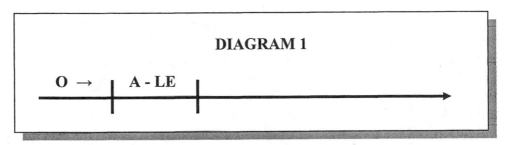

DIAGRAM 1

O →   A - LE

Because the diagram has not accounted for the whole time line, there must be a future interest following each finite estate. There are two possible future interests that can follow a finite estate. If the grantor holds the future interest following a life estate, a fee tail or a term of years, it is called a **reversion;**[69] if a third party (someone other than the grantor) holds the future interest, it is called a **remainder.**[70]

Remember, however, that a reversion and a remainder can follow only a finite possessory estate. A reversion can follow only a life estate, a fee tail, or a term of years. A remainder can follow only a life estate, a fee tail, or a term of years. **After you determine that the future interest is following one of the finite estates, then the key question to ask is "who takes the future interest?"**[71] **If the grantor holds the future interest, it is a**

---

[69] PROPERTY RESTATEMENT, *supra* note 10, at § 154, cmt. d. Just as was the case with the possibility of reverter, the common law courts ruled that because of the requirements of the livery of seisin ceremony, a grantor could *not expressly* grant a reversion to him or herself. The effect of this rule is that a reversion is *reserved* by the grantor, but at common law it could *not be expressly reserved.* Under the modern trend, followed by a majority of the jurisdictions, a reversion can be created expressly. But do not worry about memorizing this rule, because it had little practical effect. If a grantor attempted to create expressly a reversion, although it would be null and void, the grantor would take the default estate: a reversion. (One of the few areas of the law where you could not do expressly what you could do by default).

[70] PROPERTY RESTATEMENT, *supra* note 10, at § 156.

[71] Be careful. When analyzing the fee simple defeasibles, the material emphasized

reversion; if a third party holds the future interest, it is a remainder.
Remember that possessory estates and future interests go hand in hand and
should not be coupled with the wrong estates. Neither a reversion nor a
remainder would ever follow a fee simple determinable, a fee simple subject
to a condition subsequent, or a fee simple subject to an executory limitation.
Reversions and remainders follow only finite estates. Likewise, a finite estate
must be followed by a reversion or a remainder. They go hand in hand.
Coupling future interests with the appropriate preceding possessory estate
greatly facilitates the analysis.

In the big scheme of possessory estates and future interests, of the
three finite possessory estates (the life estate, the fee tail and the term of
years), the life estate is the most common and the most important for estate
planning purposes. The term of years estate is used primarily in leasehold
conveyances these days, and any further analysis or discussion of the details
of that estate is best left to that area of law. The fee tail has been abolished in
all but a handful of jurisdictions and typically shows up only on Property
exams these days.[72] Accordingly, the life estate is the most common of the
three for possessory estate and future interest purposes. Inasmuch as the
future interests following the life estate are the same as those following the
fee tail and the term of years, in discussing the future interests which go hand
in hand with the finite estates, the material will focus primarily on the life
estate. But unless noted otherwise, any example and/or rule involving a life
estate in theory applies equally well to the other two finite estates: the fee tail
and the term of years.

IV. TRANSFERABILITY, DEVISABILITY, INHERITABILITY

---

that you must ask "who takes the future interest" **before** you can determine which fee simple
defeasible it is. With the finite estates, you should ask the question "who holds the future
interest" **after** you have determined which finite possessory estate it is. With the finite
estates, you can and should determine which finite estate it is (based on the express words of
limitation) before you ask "who takes the future interest?"

[72] In adopting legislation abolishing the fee tail, the states which have abolished it are
split three ways over what interests are created if the traditional fee tail drafting language is used in
an instrument. Almost half of the state statutes deem "to A and the heirs of her body" as creating a
fee simple absolute *if* A dies survived by issue. If A dies without surviving issue, however, and if
there is an express gift over to a third party (someone other than grantor) then such gift over will be
given effect. (In essence these states construe A's interest as a fee simple determinable –
determinable if A dies without issue and there is an express gift over to a third party.) A few state
statutes deem "to A and the heirs of her body" as creating a life estate in A and A's issue take a
remainder in fee simple. MOYNIHAN, *supra* note 9, at 37-38.

In discussing the transferability, devisability, and inheritability of the finite estate,[73] the starting point is the nature of each estate. As a general rule, one cannot transfer, devise or pass through intestacy more than one has. That principle greatly affects the transferability, devisability, and inheritability of the finite estates.

Starting with the finite possessory estates, a life estate, by its nature, is not devisable or inheritable. The interest terminates upon the death of the life estate holder, so there is nothing to devise or pass through intestacy. The only question is whether it is transferable inter vivos. A life estate is transferable, but again one cannot transfer more than one owns as a general rule. If a party holding a life estate transfers that interest, the recipient receives the transferor's life estate: a life estate measured by the life of the transferor, a life estate *pur autre vie*. For example, where O grants A a life estate, and A transfers it to B, B holds a life estate measured by A's life, not B's.

Inasmuch as a fee tail is nothing more than a series of life estates, each holder of an interest under a fee tails holds nothing more than a life estate. Each party's interest will terminate upon his or her death, so it is neither devisable nor inheritable.[74] It is, however, transferable while the party is alive. But the party can transfer no more than he or she owns. The transferee would take a life estate *pur autre vie* measured by the life of the party who transferred the life estate.[75]

Absent express conditions in the conveyance creating a term of years, it is freely transferable, devisable and inheritable. For example, if O conveys a term of years for 25 years to A, A can transfer that interest while still alive, and if he or she were to die before the term were up, he or she could devise the remaining term to whomever he or she wished, and if A were to die interstate (without a will), A's heirs would inherit the remaining term.

Because reversions are vested interests, they are freely transferable, devisable, and inheritable.[76] The transferability, devisability and inheritability of remainders, on the other hand, depend upon whether they are vested or contingent – the topic of the next chapter.

---

[73] For a statement of what each of these terms mean, *see* discussion *supra* Ch. 2, IV.

[74] MOYNIHAN, *supra* note 9, at 44-45.

[75] *Id.*

[76] *Id.* at 105.

RECAP

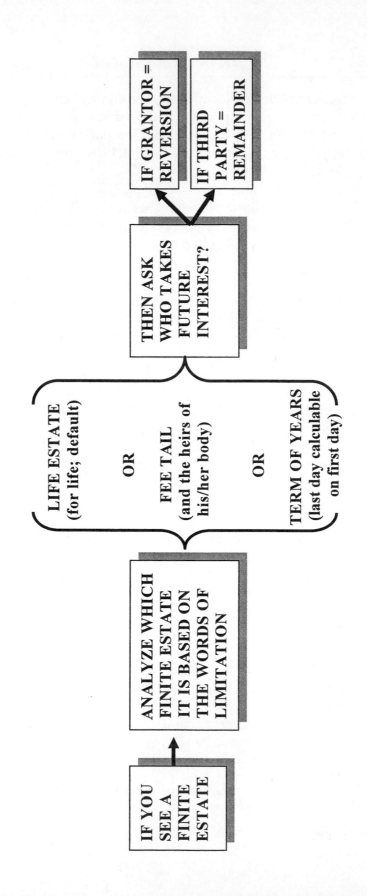

See if you can complete the following chart (use abbreviations for the different names):

CATEGORIES OF POSSESSORY ESTATES	POSSESSORY ESTATES (words of limitation)	FUTURE INTERESTS GRANTOR	THIRD PARTY
1ST : _____	(_____)	|	|
2nd : _____	(_____) (_____) (_____)	| | |	| |
3rd : _____	(_____) (_____) (_____)	| |	| | |

CATEGORIES OF POSSESSORY ESTATES	POSSESSORY ESTATES (words of limitation)	FUTURE INTERESTS GRANTOR	FUTURE INTERESTS THIRD PARTY
FEE SIMPLE ABSOLUTE	FEE SIMPLE ABSOLUTE (and her heirs)	NONE	NONE
FEE SIMPLE DEFEASIBLES	FEE SIMPLE DETERMINABLE (and her heirs as long as/while/until)	POSSIBILITY OF REVERTER	NONE
	FEE SIMPLE SUBJECT TO A CONDITION SUBEQUENT (and her heirs, but if ... right to enter)	RIGHT OF ENTRY/ POWER OF TERM	NONE
	FEE SIMPLE SUBJECT TO AN EXECUTORY LIMITATION (and her heirs as long as/but if)	NONE	EXECUTORY INTEREST (shifting vs. springing)
FINITE ESTATES	LIFE ESTATE (for life; default)	REVERSION	REMAINDER
	FEE TAIL (and the heirs of his/her body)	REVERSION	REMAINDER
	TERM OF YEARS (first & last day calculable first day)	REVERSION	REMAINDER

PROBLEM SET 3

State the title for each of the following conveyances.

1.   O →   To A for life, then to B and her heirs.

2.   O →   To A for life.

3.   O →   To A and the heirs of her body, then to B and her heirs.

4.   O →   To A and the heirs of her body.

5.   O →   To A and her heirs as long as she farms the land organically.

6.   O →   To A, then to B, and then to C and her heirs.

7.   O →   To A for 99 years.

8.   O →   To A and her heirs, then to B and her heirs.

9.   O →   To A in fee simple.

10.   O →   To A.

11.   O →   To A for ever and ever.

12.   O →   To A and her heirs, but if A hunts wildlife on the land, then to
               B and his heirs.

13.   O →   "To A for life, then to B and her heirs."

               Thereafter, A transfers her interest to C.

Chapter 5

REMAINDERS:
VESTED vs. CONTINGENT

I. OVERVIEW

Just as there are two types of executory interests – shifting and springing – there are two types of remainders: **vested** and **contingent**.[77] A remainder is the future interest which follows a life estate, fee tail or term of years *if* the future interest is held by a third party (someone other than the grantor).[78] Once you determine that a future interest is a remainder, check to see if it is vested or contingent. Contingent remainders are the default, meaning all remainders are contingent unless it qualifies as vested. If the remainder meets the test for vested, it is a vested remainder; if the remainder does not pass the test, it is a contingent remainder.

II. THE TEST FOR VESTED REMAINDERS

A remainder is vested if the remainderman (the holder of the remainder) is:

(1) **born,**
(2) **ascertainable** (i.e., you can identify the holder by his or her personal name), **and**
(3) there is **no express condition precedent**, in the clause creating the remainder or the preceding clause. (A condition precedent is one which must be satisfied *before* the remainderman can take actual possession.)[79]

---

[77] The Restatement uses the term "remainder subject to condition precedent," but that terminology has not been widely adopted and will not be used in this material. PROPERTY RESTATEMENT, *supra* note 10, at § 157.

[78] If the future interest is held by a third party but it follows a fee simple defeasible, it is an executory interest. Any time the future interest is held by a third party, there is an additional step in the analysis. It is not enough to give the basic name of the future interest. You must also give the particular subset of that future interest: shifting vs. springing; vested vs. contingent.

[79] Reading comma to comma, the express condition precedent should be set forth in the

The remainder must satisfy all three elements of the test or it is a contingent remainder.   In applying the test, *analyze the express words* creating the remainder, *reading comma to comma*, in light of the facts at the time of the conveyance.[80]

A. BORN AND ASCERTAINABLE

The first two requirements, that the remainderman must be born and ascertainable, would appear to overlap, and to a large degree they do. If the grantee is not born, how can he or she be ascertainable? But they are not identical. One can be born but not ascertainable. For example:

EXAMPLE 1

O →   To A for ten years, then to whomever is then
        President of the United States of America.

State the title. First, the estate is a finite estate. It looks like a term of years, but if the term is not calculable, the default is a life estate. Is the exact term calculable on the first day? Whatever the first day is, once it is determined then the last day can be calculated – it is ten years later. A holds a term of years.   Who holds the future interest?   Whoever is "*then*[81] President of the United States ..." – then being at the end of the ten year term.   What interest does the President hold?   Because the interest is a future interest following a term of years, and the interest is held by a third party, it is a remainder. What kind of remainder: contingent or vested? Although the person who will then be President must be alive, one cannot identify him or her by their personal name at the time of the conveyance or at the time of analysis (i.e., this moment assuming the term has not ended). Therefore, the party is not ascertainable, and the remainder is a contingent remainder. So while the first two prongs for a vested remainder, that the holder be **born** and **ascertainable**, overlap to a large degree, they are separate tests.

---

clause creating the remainder or in a preceding clause for the remainder to be contingent. If the express condition precedent is set forth in *a subsequent clause*, the remainder is a vested remainder subject to divestment. *See* discussion *infra* Ch. 7, III.

[80] And/or at the time of analysis (if later than the time of creation).

[81] Read all conveyances very, very carefully.

B. NO EXPRESS CONDITION PRECEDENT

The third prong of the vested/contingent remainder analysis is that there must be **no express condition precedent, in the same clause creating the remainder or the preceding clause**, which must be satisfied before the remainder can become possessory. If there is such an express condition precedent, the remainder is contingent until that condition is satisfied. The difference between a condition precedent and a condition subsequent is somewhat abstract, but it is critical to develop a comfort level with these terms and concepts if you are to master possessory estates and future interests.

1. Qualifying Condition Must be *Condition Precedent*

A condition precedent is a condition that applies to an interest *before* it becomes possessory. The condition precedent *must be satisfied* before the remainderman has the right to claim actual possession. In contrast, a condition subsequent is a condition which applies *after* an interest becomes possessory. The condition subsequent qualifies *how long* the possessory interest may last.

The most common example of how a condition precedent can affect a conveyance is the contingent remainder. For example:

EXAMPLE 2

O →   To A for life, then to B and her heirs if she
        graduates from law school.

State the title. A holds a life estate, and B holds a remainder in fee simple. Is the remainder vested or contingent? B is born and ascertainable, but there is an express condition in the same clause creating the remainder. Is it a condition precedent or a condition subsequent? To B and her heirs "if she graduates from law school." B gets the possessory interest (the right to take actual possession) if and only if she graduates from law school. That condition must occur *before* B's right can become possessory. It is a condition precedent – so B hold a contingent remainder.

The most common example of how a condition subsequent can affect a conveyance are the fee simple defeasibles. In the fee simple defeasibles, the express condition is always a condition subsequent. It applies to the interest *after* it becomes possessory and qualifies how long the party's right to possession may last. For example:

EXAMPLE 3

O →   To A and her heirs as long as she farms the land.

State the title. A holds the possessory interest and has the right to actual possession. But she will keep the right to possession only if she continues to farm the land. The express condition, that she farms the land, applies to her after she takes actual possession – after her interest becomes possessory. It is a condition subsequent – so A holds a fee simple determinable.

A condition precedent, and a condition subsequent, can be depicted on the time line:

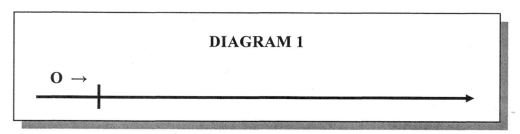

DIAGRAM 1

O →

Whether a condition is a condition precedent or a condition subsequent is determined relative to a point on the time line when the possessory estate or future interest in question is entitled to actual possession. Conceptually, as long as a condition might occur (or must occur) before the point when the party has the right to take actual possession, the condition is a condition precedent. As long as the condition can occur only after the point when the party has the right to take actual possession, the condition is a condition subsequent:

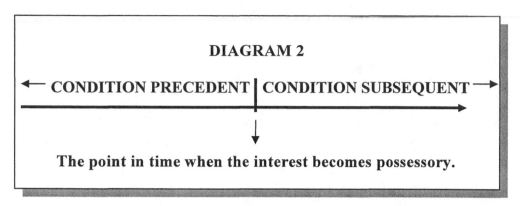

The above abstract description of what constitutes a condition precedent and a condition subsequent will make more sense when applied. For example, the above fee simple defeasible conveyance, "to A and her heirs as long as she farms the land," can be depicted on the time line:

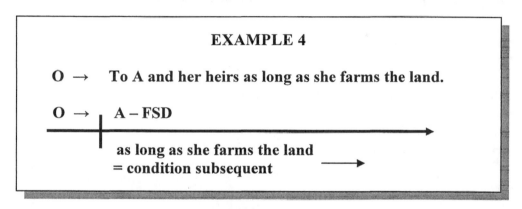

On the time line, the condition that A has the right to possession as long as she farms the land applies to the segment of the time line to the right of the cross line indicating when A's interest became possessory. It applies, if at all, to A's right to possession *after* the interest has become possessory. Thus, it is a condition subsequent.

Likewise, the above contingent remainder example, "To A for life, then to B and her heirs if she graduates from law school," can be depicted on the time line:

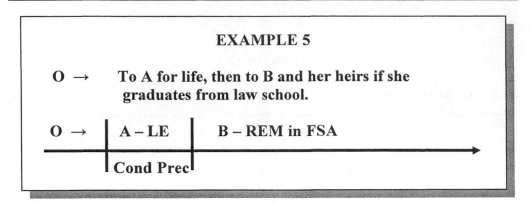

The condition that B's interest may become possessory only "if she graduates from law school" applies to the segment of the time line to the left of the cross line indicating when B's interest may become possessory (when A dies). It applies to B's right to possession *before* the interest becomes possessory. Thus, it is a condition precedent.[82]

2. Qualifying Condition Must be Express

In analyzing whether there is a condition precedent which must be satisfied before a remainder can become possessory, remember that the qualifying condition precedent must be **express**. There must be a condition set forth in **the express words of the conveyance** which must be satisfied before the holder can claim the right to possess the property. For example:

EXAMPLE 6

O →   To A for life, then to B and her heirs.

O →   To A for life, then to B and her heirs if B survives A.

O →   To A for life, then to B for life.

---

[82] If the express condition is introduced by the words "while" or "until" or "as long as" – it is almost always a condition subsequent. If an express condition is introduced by the word "if" – it is almost always a condition precedent. But be careful, if the express condition is introduced by the words "but if" – it can be either a condition precedent or a condition subsequent. Careful attention to the nature of the condition is necessary to analyze whether it is a condition precedent or a condition subsequent.

State the titles. In all three conveyances, A has a life estate. Because the future interest following the life estate is held by B, a third party, in all three conveyances the future interest is a remainder. Is it a vested or contingent remainder? B is an abbreviation for a person's personal name, so B must be alive and ascertainable.[83] The question is whether there is an **express** condition precedent in the language of the conveyance, either in the same clause creating the remainder or in a preceding clause, which must be satisfied before B can claim actual possession of the property at the end of A's possessory estate.

In the first conveyance, there is no express condition precedent and B holds a vested remainder. While it is true that B has to survive A if B personally is to take actual possession of the property, because B holds a **vested** remainder in **fee simple absolute** (as opposed to a life estate) B does not have to survive A to have the right to take possession of the property when A's life estate ends. Even if B were to predecease A, the vested remainder in fee simple absolute is still B's property and would pass into her probate estate to be distributed to B's devisees or heirs, depending on whether B dies testate (with a will) or intestate (without a will). Because B holds a vested remainder in fee simple, B's death would not affect B's vested right to possess the property at the end of A's life estate.[84]

In the second conveyance, there is an express condition precedent - an express condition which must be satisfied **before** B can take possession of the property (at the end of A's life estate). The language of the conveyance expressly provides that B is to have the right to possess the land only if B survives A. There is an express condition which must be satisfied before B will be entitled to claim *actual* possession of the property – *before* B's interest can become possessory. Thus, B holds a contingent remainder.

In the third conveyance, B holds a remainder in life estate. For B's life estate to be worth anything, as a practical matter, B must survive A. Does that make B's life estate contingent? No. The condition precedent

---

[83] Always assume that a person identified by a letter is alive unless the facts of the problem tell you otherwise. *See* discussion *supra* fn. 1.

[84] Although if all the party held was a vested remainder *in life estate*, if the party died before the preceding estate ended, the vested remainder would expire before the party had the chance to possess the land. But that is because of the inherent nature of a life estate, not because of an express condition precedent, which deprived the party holding the remainder of their right to possession.

must be an **express** condition, not one implicit in the nature of the estate (or the words of limitation). There is no express condition precedent in this conveyance, just an express life estate. Thus, B holds a vested remainder in life estate.

3. Qualifying Condition Must be in Same Clause or Preceding Clause

If there is an express condition precedent, it must be in the *same clause* as the clause creating the remainder or *the preceding clause* for the remainder to be contingent. This requirement is derived from the historical evolution of possessory estates and future interests. Prior to the Statute of Uses in 1536, the common law rule was that if a party held a vested remainder, the party could not lose the right to possession before taking actual possession. Pre-1536, if the conveyance contained an express condition precedent, but the condition precedent was in the clause *after* the clause creating the remainder, the remainder was deemed vested and the express condition was null and void. Therefore, to indicate clearly that the remainder's right to take possession was conditioned on the occurrence of the express condition precedent, the express condition precedent had to be in the same clause creating the remainder or the preceding clause.

Today, if the express condition precedent is in a clause subsequent to the clause creating the remainder, the condition is not null and void, but it creates a new combination of estates which the material will examine later.[85] For now, just remember that for the condition precedent to make the remainder contingent, it must be set forth in the same clause creating the remainder or the preceding clause.

4. Recap

By default, all remainders are contingent remainders unless they meet the test for vested. A remainder is vested if the party holding the remainder is (a) born, (b) ascertainable, and (c) *there is no* express condition precedent in the same clause creating the remainder or the preceding clause. If any of these requirements is not satisfied, the remainder or the preceding clause, the remainder is contingent.

---

[85] *See* discussion *infra* Ch. 7, III.

III. DESTRUCTIBILITY OF CONTINGENT REMAINDERS

The distinction between the vested and contingent remainder is important for several reasons. The most important reason is the **common law rule of destructibility of contingent remainders**. **At common law, a contingent remainder had to vest at, or prior to, the end of the preceding finite estate, or the contingent remainder was destroyed by operation of law**. The significance of the destructibility of contingent remainder rule can be demonstrated through the following example:

EXAMPLE 7

O → To A for life, then to B and her heirs if B survives A.

State the title. A holds a finite estate, a life estate. The future interest is in B, a third party, so it must be a remainder. The words of limitation "and her heirs" indicate that the remainder is in fee simple. Is the remainder vested or contingent? There is an express condition in the same clause as the clause creating the remainder. Is it a condition precedent or subsequent? It is introduced by the word "if" and requires B to survive A for B's interest to become possessory. That requirement must be satisfied either before, or at the moment, A's life estate ends. Thus, the condition is a condition precedent.

B holds a contingent remainder, contingent on B surviving A. If B dies before A, under the common law destructibility of contingent remainders, the contingent remainder is destroyed. The contingent remainder must vest, if at all, prior to or at the moment the preceding finite estate ends or it is destroyed. Here, if B dies before A, the express condition precedent cannot be satisfied so B's interest is destroyed. B loses all interest in the property; B's contingent remainder is destroyed before it becomes possessory. Who then would take the property?

Anytime there is a contingent remainder, there must be someone to take the property if the contingent remainder fails to vest in time and is destroyed. Where there is no express party to take in case the contingent remainder fails to vest, the default taker is always the

original grantor.[86] Because the grantor (O) would take the property after the finite possessory estate (A's life estate), the grantor (O) holds a future interest. Because the future interest follows the life estate and the grantor holds it, the grantor holds a reversion (and because it is a "default"[87] reversion, it is in fee simple absolute). Returning to example 7 for a moment, the full state of the title is:

EXAMPLE 7A

O →   To A for life, then to B and her heirs if B survives A.

A has a life estate;
B has a contingent remainder in fee simple, and
O has a reversion in fee simple.

If the express condition precedent is not satisfied either prior to or at the moment finite estate ends (i.e., if B's contingent remainder does not vest prior to or at the moment A's life estate ends), the contingent remainder is destroyed by operation of law under the common law rule of destructibility of contingent remainders. If B dies before A's life estate ends, when A dies, O's reversion becomes possessory, and O would hold the property in fee simple absolute.

If, however, the contingent remainder were one which could vest before the end of the preceding estate, the analysis is slightly different. For example:

EXAMPLE 8

O →   To A for life, then to B and her heirs if B graduates from
       law school.

---

[86] MOYNIHAN, *supra* note 9, at 133-134.

[87] It is a default reversion in the sense that it is not express. The term "default" reversion is not a recognized term of art under the common law terminology. Nevertheless, many students find it helpful to call it a default reversion, and technically there should be nothing wrong with calling it a default reversion because the term "default" describes how it is created. But technically a default reversion is just a reversion, and when stating the title should be called just a reversion.

State the title. A holds a finite estate, a life estate. The future interest following the finite estate is held by a third party, B, so it is a remainder. The remainder is in fee simple because of the words of limitation "and her heirs … ." Is the remainder vested or contingent? There is an express condition in the same clause as the clause creating the remainder. Is it a condition precedent or a condition subsequent? It is a condition precedent because it is introduced by the word "if" and it requires B to graduate from law school before B's right can become possessory.

B holds a contingent remainder, contingent on B graduating from law school. Just as above, if the express condition precedent is not satisfied either prior to or at the moment A's life estate ends, the contingent remainder is destroyed pursuant to the common law destructibility of contingent remainders. If, however, two years after this conveyance and while A is still alive, B graduates from law school, the express condition precedent has now been satisfied. B is born, ascertainable, and the express condition precedent has been satisfied. The remainder is now vested. Because it is vested, there is no longer any need for the default taker, and O's reversion is extinguished. The state of the title would simply be: A has a life estate, and B has a vested remainder in fee simple. Thus, remainders have to be analyzed not only in light of the facts at the time the conveyance is executed, but also in light of subsequent factual developments all the way up to the moment of analysis. As long as the remainder vests before the end of the preceding finite estate or at the moment it ends, the default reversion in O is extinguished.[88]

Contingent remainders can be diagramed. First, return to Example 7 as it was originally drafted:

EXAMPLE 7

O →   To A for life, then to B and her heirs if B survives A.

A has a life estate;
B has a contingent remainder in fee simple, and
O has a reversion in fee simple.

---

[88] So is O's reversion called a *contingent* reversion, or *a possibility of* reversion, to reflect the fact that it may not become possessory? No. This point is implicitly reflected in the fact that it is a default reversion following a contingent remainder. It is still a reversion and has all the other characteristics of a reversion (in particular, it is transferable).

First, diagram A's life estate:

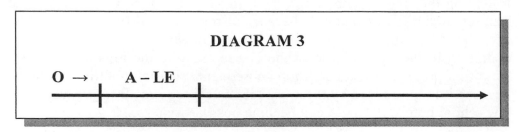

What about the contingent remainder and the default reversion? Although there are several possible ways to diagram the relationship between these two estates, two key characteristics dictate the better way to diagram them. First, because the remainder is **contingent**, it should be depicted by a dashed line as opposed to a solid line.[89] Second, because of the destructibility of contingent remainders, the contingent remainder exists only as long as there is a supporting finite estate. Thus, for purposes of diagramming the contingent remainder, **a bold** solid cross line indicating the end of the supporting finite estate becomes something of a vertical support (or "crane") holding up the contingent remainder:

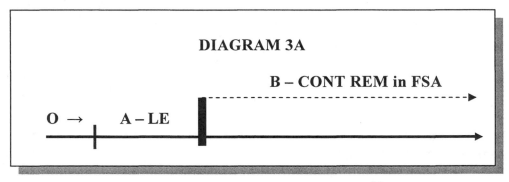

As always, the reversion is depicted as a solid line[90] on the time line following the finite estate:

---

[89] The dashed line is used to show the tenuous, "iffy" nature of the interest. Remember the dashed line was also used to depict the possibility that the fee simple *may* end in the fee simple defeasible graphs.

[90] All reversions are vested interests. LEWIS M. SIMES, SIMES ON FUTURE INTERESTS 25 (West Publishing 1951).

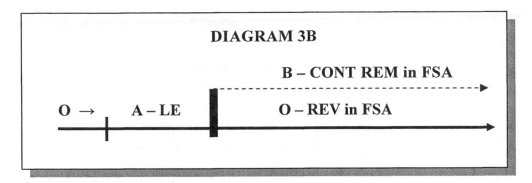

What if the contingent remainder vests prior to the end of the supporting finite estate? Return to Example 8:

EXAMPLE 8

O → To A for life, then to B and her heirs if B graduates from law school.

State the title. A has a life estate, B has a contingent remainder in fee simple, and O has a reversion in fee simple. Diagram the title:

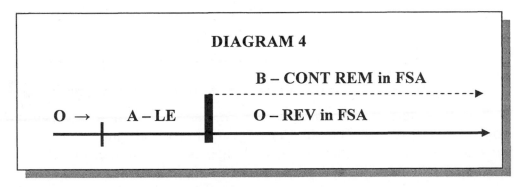

Now assume the facts go on to state that B graduates from law school (while A is still alive). The moment B graduates from law school, the express condition precedent is satisfied. Now B is born, ascertainable, and there is no longer an express condition precedent to B's interest becoming possessory. If the contingent remainder vests prior to the end of the supporting finite estate (or the moment it ends), the moment the remainder vests it is lowered down the "crane" onto the arrow, displacing the reversion. Because the remainder has become vested, it no longer is a dashed line. It is on the solid time line:

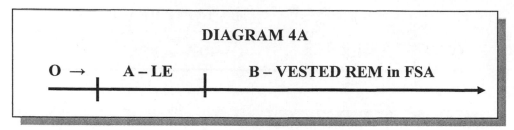

If, on the other hand, the supporting life estate ends prior to the contingent remainder vesting, the contingent remainder no longer has a supporting vertical beam, and it is destroyed pursuant to the destructibility of contingent remainders. For example, in Example 6 above, assume the facts went on to state the A died a month before B was scheduled to graduate from law school. The express contingent precedent could no longer be satisfied during the preceding finite estate, so B's contingent remainder would be destroyed pursuant to the destructibility of contingent remainders. O's reversion would then become possessory, and O would hold the property in fee simple absolute:

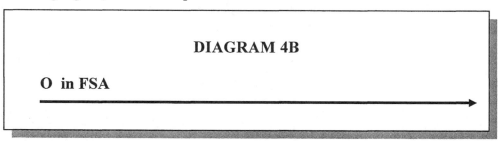

Notice O would not hold a *reversion* in fee simple absolute because the moment A died and B's contingent remainder had not vested, O's reversion became possessory. It is no longer is a future interest. O holds the property in fee simple absolute.

IV. ALTERNATIVE CONTINGENT REMAINDERS

A. INTRODUCTION

The final twist on contingent remainders concerns the **alternative contingent remainder**. Alternative contingent remainders arise where the conveyance sets forth two contingent remainders, and the second one is contingent on the first failing to vest. For example:

EXAMPLE 9

O → To A for life, then to B and her heirs if B graduates from law school, but if B fails to graduate from law school, then to C and her heirs.

State the title. A has a life estate. The future interest is in B, a third party, so B has a remainder. The words of limitation "and her heirs" indicates that B holds her remainder in fee simple. The express condition precedent in the same clause as the clause creating the remainder indicates that B's interest is a contingent remainder in fee simple.

C's interest is a future interest which, if it were to become possessory, would follow A's life estate.[91] Thus, C's interest must be a remainder (a future interest following a finite estate – A's life estate – held by a third party – C). The express words of limitation "and her heirs" indicates that it is a remainder in fee simple absolute. The more difficult question is whether it is contingent or vested. The language of the conveyance expressly provides that C's interest is to become possessory **only** if B's interest fails ("if B fails to graduate from law school"). That constitutes an express condition precedent which must occur before C's interest can become possessory. Thus, C has **an alternative contingent remainder** in fee simple absolute. It is an **alternative** contingent remainder because it will become possessory only if another contingent remainder does not. Where there are alternative contingent remainders, is there a default reversion in the grantor?

The key to analyzing O's interest is to diagram the state of the title. A's life estate is easy enough, for it is the first segment on the time line - it is a vested interest:

---

[91] C's interest will become possessory only if B's contingent remainder does not vest. Thus, C will take possession, if at all, following A's life estate.

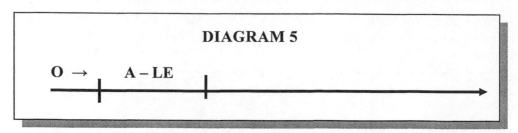

DIAGRAM 5

O →   A – LE

B's interest, because it is a contingent remainder, is depicted as a dotted line secured to the top of the bolded cross line depicting the end of A's life estate:

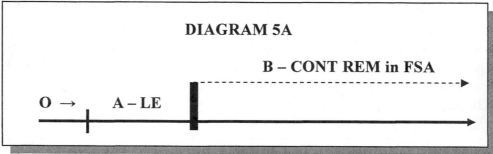

DIAGRAM 5A

B – CONT REM in FSA

O →   A – LE

C's interest, because it is an alternative contingent remainder, is likewise depicted as a dotted line secured to the bolded cross line depicting the end of the life estate:

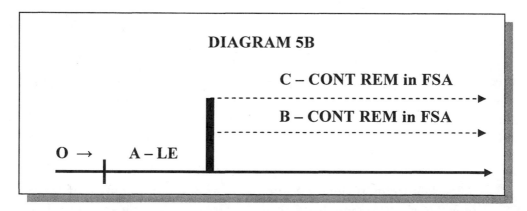

DIAGRAM 5B

C – CONT REM in FSA

B – CONT REM in FSA

O →   A – LE

The problem is that state of the title does not account for the whole time line. It fails to account for the rest of the time line following the life estate (until one of the contingent remainders vests). The default taker is always the grantor – O. Because it is a future interest held by the grantor following a life estate, it is a reversion; and because it is the rest of the time line, and it is a default reversion, it is in fee simple absolute.

That accounts for the whole time line. The full state of the title is: A has a life estate, B has a contingent remainder in fee simple, and O holds a reversion in fee simple. The full state of the title can be depicted on the time line as follows:

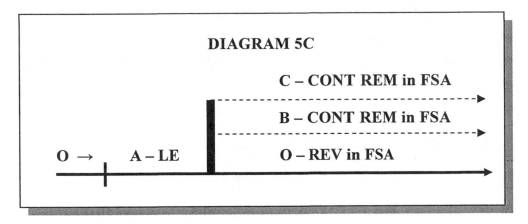

DIAGRAM 5C

C – CONT REM in FSA

B – CONT REM in FSA

O →   A – LE   O – REV in FSA

B. ALTERNATIVE PHRASING

There are two ways to phrase alternative contingent remainders. The first is the wording used in example above 8 (restated in Example 9 below) where the alternative contingent remainder is preceded by an *express* clause stating that the alternative remainder is contingent upon the first remainder not meeting its express condition precedent. There is, however, a more subtle way of stating the same condition precedent. For example:

EXAMPLE 10

O → To A for life, then to B and her heirs if B graduates from law school, but if B fails to graduate from law school, then to C and her heirs.

O → To A for life, then to B and her heirs if B graduates from law school, otherwise to C and her heirs.

In the second conveyance, the word "otherwise" serves the same function as the express clause in the first conveyance stating that the alternative remainder is contingent upon the first remainder not meeting its express condition precedent. Watch for either phrasing of alternative contingent remainders.

C. ALTERNATIVE CONTINGENT REMAINDER LOOK-ALIKE

One more conveyance should be noted. Up until now, all of our contingent remainder examples have involved contingent remainders **in fee simple**. Where the first contingent remainder is **not** in fee simple, there can be an express gift over to a third party in fee simple which eliminates any need for a default reversion in the grantor. For example:

EXAMPLE 11

O →   To A for life, then to B for life if B graduates from
       law school, but if B fails to graduate from law school,
       then to C and her heirs.

State the title. At first blush the conveyance looks like a set of classic alternative contingent remainders, but upon closer analysis it is not. A has a life estate. But B has a contingent remainder but only in life estate, not in fee simple. If that were all the conveyance expressly provided for, O would have a default reversion whether B's contingent remainder became possessory or not. But in Example 11, the conveyance grants an express future interest to C. C's interest will follow either A or B's life estate, so it is a remainder. The express words of limitation "and her heirs" indicate it is a remainder in fee simple. And there is no express condition precedent qualifying C's right to take possession so it is vested. Because there is a vested remainder in fee simple, there is no need for a default reversion in the grantor.

The conveyance can be diagramed as follows:

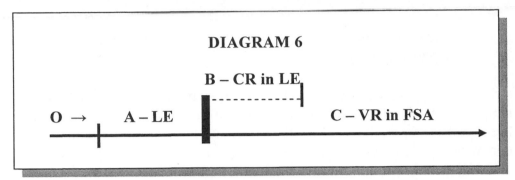

DIAGRAM 6

B's remainder is of finite duration so it is a short line segment with a definite end point. B's remainder is contingent so it is a dotted line segment. Again, because it is contingent, it is secured to and dependent upon the supporting life estate in A. If the facts went on to state that during A's lifetime B graduated from law school, B's remainder would vest. Schematically, the life estate would be lowered down the supporting crane and inserted on the time line between the two vested interests (A's life estate and C's vested remainder in fee simple). Because B's interest is only a finite estate, it would not displace any interest:

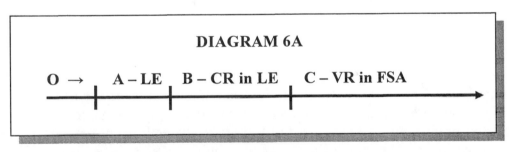

DIAGRAM 6A

If, on the other hand, A were to die *before* B graduated from law school, the destructibility of contingent remainders would apply and B's contingent remainder would be destroyed. C's vested remainder in fee simple would become possessory.

So where the conveyance transfers a contingent remainder of a finite estate *and* a vested remainder in fee simple, there is no alternative contingent remainder and thus there is no default reversion.

V. PREMATURE TERMINATION OF FINITE ESTATE

A. METHODS BY WHICH FINITE ESTATE MAY END PREMATURELY

The analysis of the destructibility of contingent remainders is rather simple and straightforward where the supporting finite estate[92] ends naturally (i.e., typically upon the death of the life estate holder). For example, in the conveyance "To A for life, then to B and her heirs if she graduates from law school," A holds a life estate, B holds a contingent remainder in fee simple, and O holds a (default) reversion in fee simple. If A were to die before B graduates from law school, B's contingent remainder would be destroyed, and O's reversion would become possessory.

There are, however, three other ways in which a finite estate may end prematurely: **forfeiture, renunciation,** and **merger.**   Moreover, the common law destructibility of contingent remainders (that the contingent remainder must vest at or prior to the end of the preceding estate or it is deemed destroyed by operation of law), applies with equal force to the three ways in which a finite estate may end prematurely.

1. Forfeiture

At common law, if a life tenant[93] committed certain crimes, the punishment could include **forfeiture.** Forfeiture terminated the life tenant's life estate interest in the property. If the contingent remainder had not vested prior to or at the moment of forfeiture, the contingent remainder was destroyed, and the grantor's reversion would become possessory. This method of prematurely terminating a finite estate, however, is extremely rare today because society no longer recognizes forfeiture to the same degree as it did at common law.[94]

2. Renunciation

A life tenant can voluntarily **renounce** their interest in the life estate

---

[92] Typically the supporting finite estate is a life estate. The discussion will assume that the underlying finite estate is a life estate, but it need not be.

[93] The holder of the life estate.

[94] Although some jurisdictions still use forfeiture in connection with certain crimes, for example drug dealing.

at any time during the life estate. The effect of a renunciation is to terminate the party's interest in the property as of the moment of the renunciation. If there is a contingent remainder and it has not vested by the time of, or at the moment of, renunciation, the contingent remainder will be destroyed under the rule of the destructibility of contingent remainders.

3. Merger

The third and final way a life estate[95] can end prematurely is by **merger**. The doctrine of merger provides that if the same party holds successive vested interests, the interests should be merged and re-identified based upon the largest estate created by the merger. There are several points to note about the merger doctrine. First, merger applies **only** to vested interests.[96] Second, for the merger doctrine to apply the vested interests must be **successive** and **held by the same party.**

The time line diagram greatly facilitates understanding the merger doctrine. First, an example:

EXAMPLE 12

O → To A for life, then to B and her heirs.

State the title. A has a life estate, B has a vested remainder in fee simple. Diagram the title:

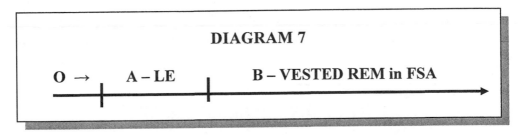

DIAGRAM 7

O →   A – LE   B – VESTED REM in FSA

---

[95] Or fee tail or terms of years, as the case may be.
[96] All possessory estates are vested, but only reversions and vested remainders are vested. Vested interests are those depicted on the time line diagram *on* the time line.

What if while A were alive, A transferred A's life estate to B?[97] B would now hold the life estate (*pur autre vie*) and the vested remainder in fee simple absolute.

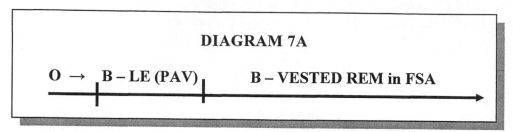

DIAGRAM 7A

O → B – LE (PAV)   B – VESTED REM in FSA

B now holds the possessory interest and the only future interest. B holds the whole time line. If one owns the whole time line, one holds a fee simple absolute.   Therefore, under the doctrine of merger, the life estate would merge into the remainder (two successive vested interests held by the same party) to create a fee simple absolute in B:

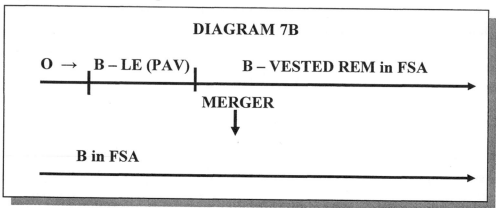

DIAGRAM 7B

O → B – LE (PAV)   B – VESTED REM in FSA

MERGER

B in FSA

For merger to apply, however, the vested interests must be successive. There cannot be another vested interest in between them. For example:

EXAMPLE 13

O → To A for life, then to B for life, then to C and her heirs.

---

[97] Merger typically comes into play when a finite estate is transferred. Merger may also apply, however, if a fee simple defeasible is transferred back to the grantor. But this scenario is much less common than the transfer of a finite estate.

State the title. A has a life estate. The future interest is in a third party, B, so B holds a remainder. The express words of limitation, "for life," indicate that B's remainder is in life estate. Is the remainder vested or contingent? Reading comma to comma, B is born, ascertainable, and there is no express condition precedent in the same clause creating the remainder or the preceding clause, so the remainder is vested. B holds a vested remainder in life estate. Because B's vested remainder is only a life estate, and not a fee simple absolute, there must be a future interest after B's interest. Here, that interest is express – C holds the future interest following B's life estate. Because B's possessory interest is a life estate, the future interest following it must be a reversion or a remainder. Because C holds the future interest following B's interest, it must be a remainder. The express words of limitation describing C's interest, "and her heirs," indicates that C's remainder is in fee simple absolute. Is it vested or contingent? Reading comma to comma (or in this clause, comma to the end of the conveyance), C is born, ascertainable, and there is no express condition precedent in the same clause creating the remainder or the preceding clause, so the remainder is vested. C holds a vested remainder in fee simple absolute.[98]

The state of the title can be diagrammed:

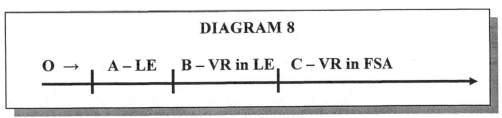

DIAGRAM 8

O → | A – LE | B – VR in LE | C – VR in FSA

Now assume A transfers her life estate to C. Does the merger doctrine apply?

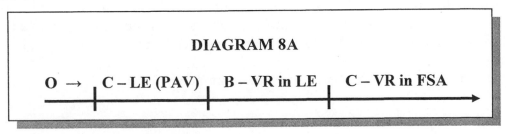

DIAGRAM 8A

O → | C – LE (PAV) | B – VR in LE | C – VR in FSA

---

[98] O, the original grantor, holds nothing. There is no need for a default reversion as O has transferred all that he or she owned.

Merger does not apply. The merger doctrine permits lesser estates to be merged into a greater estate if the same party holds successive vested interests. Although C holds two vested interests (a vested remainder in fee simple absolute and a life estate *pur autre vie*), the interests are not successive. B's vested remainder in life estate is in between.

Merger is relevant to contingent remainders because the effect of merger is to terminate the lesser estate, typically a life estate.[99] Coupling the merger doctrine with the common law destructibility of contingent remainders, when a supporting life estate ends prematurely through merger, if the contingent remainder has not vested prior to or at the moment the life estate ends, the contingent remainder is destroyed. For example, return to Example 8:

EXAMPLE 8

O → To A for life, then to B and her heirs if B graduates from law school.

State the title. A has a life estate. The future interest must be a reversion or a remainder. Because B, a third party holds it, the future interest must be a remainder. The words of limitation "and her heirs" indicate that B holds a remainder in fee simple. Is it a fee simple defeasible? There is qualifying language *after* the fee simple words of limitation. But here the qualifying language introduces an express condition *precedent* – "*if* B graduates from law school." For the estate to be fee simple defeasible, the qualifying language has to introduce an express condition *subsequent*. So B holds a remainder in fee simple. But is the remainder vested or contingent? As just mentioned, there is an express condition precedent in the same clause creating the remainder, so B holds a contingent remainder in fee simple. Because B's remainder is contingent, there must be a default taker in case B's interest does not vest before the end of the preceding life estate. O holds a reversion in fee simple.

The state of the title can be diagrammed:

---

[99] Or other finite estate, as the case may be.

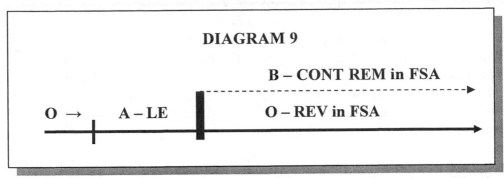

Now assume the problem went on to tell you that while A was still alive and before B graduated from law school, A transferred her life estate to O (or, conversely, if O transferred her reversion in fee simple to A), one party would hold successive vested interests so the merger doctrine would apply to create a fee simple absolute. If either of those transfers were to occur, because the contingent remainder had not vested before the end of the life estate, it would be destroyed by the combined effect of the merger doctrine and the destructibility of contingent remainders. On the other hand, if the problem went on to tell you that while A was still alive, B graduated from law school, the remainder would vest and the default reversion in O would be extinguished.

Anytime there is a contingent remainder, there should be a default reversion in the grantor. Anytime one party transfers his or her interest to another party who already holds an interest, check to see if merger applies.

B. APPLICATION TO ALTERNATIVE CONTINGENT REMAINDERS

The twist on the alternative contingent remainder is that as long as the first contingent remainder has not vested, both contingent remainders are subject to the rule of destructibility of contingent remainders through either merger, renunciation or forfeiture. Assuming a standard alternative contingent remainder state of the title (life estate, contingent remainder in fee simple, alternative remainder in fee simple, and reversion in fee simple),[100] if the life transfers her life estate to the grantor, or if the grantor

---

[100] For example: "To A for life, then to B and her heirs if B graduates from law school, but if B fails to graduate from law school, then to C and her heirs."

transfers her reversion in fee simple to the life tenant, the resulting fee simple absolute through merger would destroy **both** contingent remainders. In the alternative, if the life tenant were to renounce her interest, the result would be the same – both contingent remainders would be destroyed; as they would be if the life tenant committed a crime which carried the punishment of forfeiture. Premature termination of the underlying finite estate often has harsh consequences in the alternative contingent remainder setting.

The key then to analyzing alternative contingent remainders is to focus on how the preceding finite estate ends.   Anytime there are alternative contingent remainders, if the preceding finite estate ends **prematurely (through merger, renunciation or forfeiture), only the reversion or the first possessory estate can become possessory.** If the first contingent remainder has not vested prior to or at the moment the finite estate ends **prematurely,** both of the contingent remainders are destroyed and the reversion becomes possessory. If, on the other hand, the first contingent remainder **has** vested by the premature termination of the preceding finite estate, upon the vesting of the first contingent remainder, the alternative contingent remainder and the reversion are destroyed.

If, however, there are alternative contingent remainders and the preceding finite estate ends **naturally,** there is no chance that the default reversion will become possessory.   The only issue is whether the first contingent remainder has vested.   If the first contingent remainder has vested prior to or at the moment the finite estate ends naturally, the first finite estate will become possessory and the alternative contingent remainder and the reversion in O are destroyed. On the other hand, if the preceding finite estate ends naturally and the first contingent remainder has **not** vested prior to or at the moment the finite estate ends naturally, the first contingent remainder will fail (and will be destroyed under the destructibility of contingent remainders) and the alternative contingent remainder will become possessory. Notice, if the preceding finite estate ends naturally, one of the two alternative contingent remainders will become possessory and the reversion will be destroyed. Which of the two contingent remainders will become possessory depends upon whether the first contingent remainder vests prior to or at the moment of the natural expiration of the preceding finite estate.

VI. TRANSFERABILITY, DEVISABILITY AND INHERITABILITY

Vested remainders are also freely transferable, devisable, and inheritable to the extent permitted by the express terms of the conveyance and/or the nature of the possessory duration of the future interest.[101] For example, if O conveyed the property "To A for life, then to B for life, then to C and her heirs," B holds a vested remainder in life estate. Although in theory B's vested remainder is freely transferable, devisable, and inheritable, because it is a vested remainder in life estate, if B were to die before A, the interest would terminate upon B's death – thereby making it not devisable or inheritable. But because C's vested remainder is in fee simple, it is freely transferable, devisable, and inheritable, even if C were to die before the interest becomes possessory.

On the other hand, the common law courts viewed contingent remainders with disfavor. The future interest is, after all, *contingent* – uncertain. Accordingly, the common law courts decreed that contingent remainders were not transferable.[102] But contingent remainders were devisable and inheritable to the extent the nature of the express condition precedent and the duration of the future interest permit.[103] For example, if O were to convey the property "To A for life, then to B and her heirs if A graduates from law school," if B were to die, the future interest would not terminate upon A's death. If A were to graduate from law school after B's death, the remainder would vest. And because B's contingent remainder is in fee simple, the interest still has value after B's death. B's contingent remainder is not transferable while B is alive, but it is devisable and inheritable upon B's death. On the other hand, if O's conveyance read "To A for life, then to B for life if A graduates from law school," upon B's death B's interest would terminate because it was only a life estate measured by B's life. In addition, if O's conveyance read "To A for life, then to B and her heirs if B survives A," although B's contingent remainder is in fee simple, because the express condition is that B must survive A, upon B's death before A, the interest would be destroyed under the destructibility of contingent remainders and would not be devisable or inheritable.

In summary, at common law all possessory estates and future interests were transferable, devisable, and inheritable to the extent permitted by the

---

[101] MOYNIHAN, *supra* note 9, at 139.

[102] *Id.*

[103] *Id.* at 140.

nature of the estate (i.e., its duration), with the exception of (1) the possibility of reverter and right of entry/power of termination, which were not transferable or devisable, and (2) the contingent remainders and executory interests,[104] which were not transferable.[105]

---

[104] Executory interests were non-transferable until the end of the sixteenth century. POWELL, *supra* note 57, ¶ 283 at 252.

[105] If is very important that you practice analyzing as many conveyances as possible. There are two problem sets after the next chapter. The next chapter is a short chapter designed primarily to help with the mechanics of how to analyze a conveyance. If you feel you are ready, you can try to analyze the conveyances in Problem Sets 4 and 5 at this point.

Chapter 6

ALTERNATIVE APPROACH FOR ANALYZING CONVEYANCES: LEAD WITH THE PARTIES

I. OVERVIEW

Although the analysis of the basic possessory estates and future interests started out simply enough, by now the material has conveyed a sense of the complexity and myriad combinations which may be possible. Remember the process of stating the title is a multiple step process.

First, analyze the possessory interest. For the possessory estate: (1) identify **who** holds the possessory interest (focus on the **words of purchase**); and (2) identify **which possessory estate** the party holds (first identify which category of possessory estates it is in and then focus on the **words of limitation** in the clause creating the possessory estate to determine which possessory estate it is).

For each future interest, the analysis is a three step process (1) identify **who** holds the future interest (focus on the **words of purchase** at the beginning of the future interest clause); (2) **identify which future interest it is** - that should flow automatically from (a) your classification of the **immediately preceding** possessory estate, and (b) "**who holds**" the future interest – the grantor or a third party; and (3) state the **duration** of the future interest (focus on the **words of limitation** in the clause creating the future interest).

II.   ALTERNATIVE APPROACH: LEAD WITH THE PARTIES

A slightly different approach is to identify all of the parties named in the conveyance who could have a property interest in the conveyance (including the grantor) and to list them. For example, start with the following conveyance:

EXAMPLE 1

O →   To A for life, then to B for life, then to C and the heirs
of her body.

There are four parties who could possibly hold an interest:

EXAMPLE 1A

A:
B:
C:
and O:

Having listed all of the parties who *may* have a property interest, the task is simply to identify the property interest of each, if any.

In identifying the property interest of each, remember that the first party, the party holding the possessory interest,[106] will have only one phrase describing his or her property interest (because the name of the possessory estate and its duration are one and the same). In contrast, all the other parties holding a property interest must have two phrases describing their property interest: first, the name of the future interest (which depends on the possessory estate it follows), and second, the duration of the future interest (which turns on the express words of limitation in the clause creating that future interest):

EXAMPLE 1B

A: holds a _____ (possessory estate),
B: holds a _____ (future interest) in _____ (possessory estate),
C: holds a _____ (future interest) in _____ (possessory estate),
& O: ?

---

[106] There is one situation in which the first party named in the conveyance will not hold the possessory estate – but that estate combination is to come. *See* discussion *infra* Ch. 7, II, A.

O may or may not hold a future interest depending on whether the last express grantee holds a vested future interest in fee simple absolute. In our example, if C holds a vested future interest in fee simple, O will hold nothing. But if C does not, O is the default taker of the remaining future interest in fee simple absolute.

Now, looking at the express language of the conveyance, the words of limitation "for life" after the words of purchase "to A" indicates that A has a life estate:

EXAMPLE 1C

A: holds a <u>life estate,</u>
B: holds a _____ (future interest) in _____ (possessory estate),
C: holds a _____ (future interest) in _____ (possessory estate),
& O: ?

Inasmuch as A holds a life estate, the future interest following it must be either a reversion or a remainder. Because B holds it, the future interest must be a remainder. Of what duration? The express words of limitation in the clause creating B's remainder are "for life", so B holds a remainder in life estate. Is B's remainder vested or contingent? B is born, ascertainable and there is no express condition precedent, so it is vested:

EXAMPLE 1D

A: holds a <u>life estate,</u>
B: holds a <u>vested remainder</u> in <u>life estate,</u>
C: holds a _____ (future interest) in _____ (possessory estate),
& O: ?

Inasmuch as B holds a life estate, the future interest following it must be either a reversion or a remainder. Because C holds it, it must be a remainder. Of what duration? The express words of limitation in the clause creating C's remainder are "and the heirs of her body" so C holds a remainder in fee tail. Is C's remainder vested or contingent? C is born, ascertainable and there is no express condition precedent, so it is vested:

EXAMPLE 1E

A: holds a <u>life estate,</u>
B: holds a   <u>vested remainder</u> in <u>life estate,</u>
C: holds a   <u>vested remainder</u> in <u>fee tail,</u>
& O: ?

Does O hold any interest? If we were to diagram the conveyance, have we accounted for the whole time line? :

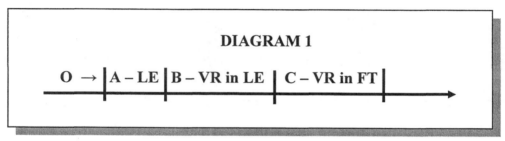

DIAGRAM 1

O →   A – LE   B – VR in LE   C – VR in FT

No, C's remainder in fee tail does not account for the end of the time line.

Another way to think about whether O has a default interest without diagramming the conveyance is to ask whether the last express future interest is in fee simple absolute? If the answer is "no," then you have not accounted for the whole time line, and O must hold a reversion in fee simple absolute. If the answer is yes, but the future interest is a **contingent** remainder in fee simple, you still have to give O a default reversion in fee simple. Returning to our example, because C holds a vested remainder but only in fee tail, not fee simple absolute, the state of the title so far has not accounted for the whole time line. The courts will imply that O reserved a reversion in fee simple absolute:

EXAMPLE 1F

A: holds a <u>life estate,</u>
B: holds a <u>vested remainder</u> in <u>life estate,</u>
C: holds a   <u>vested remainder</u> in <u>fee tail,</u>
& O: holds a <u>reversion</u> in <u>fee simple absolute.</u>

By including O in each of your lists of potential takers it will force you to think about whether you have accounted for the **whole** fee simple absolute in stating the title to the conveyance.

One last point that should help you analyze conveyances. Notice that with the finite possessory estates, there can be (and often are) more than one future interest. Future interests following a finite estate can be combined (or "stacked") in all sorts of different combinations. In contrast, with the fee simple defeasibles (the fee simple determinable, the fee simple subject to a condition subsequent, and the fee simple subject to an executory limitation), only one future interest can follow the fee simple defeasible possessory estates (and it will be in fee simple duration).

PROBLEM SET 4

State the complete title for the following problems.

1.   O →   To A for life, then to B and her heirs.

A has a _____ ,

B has a _____ **in** _____ ,

O has ? _____ .

2.   O →   To A for life, then to B and the heirs of her body, then to
        C and his heirs.

A has a _____ ,

B has a _____ **in** _____ ,

C has a _____ **in** _____ ,

O has ? _____ .

3.   O →   To A and the heirs of her body, then to B for life, then to C
        and her heirs as long as maintains the wetlands on the
        property.

A has a _____ ,

B has a _____ **in** _____ ,

C has a _____ **in** _____ ,

O has ? _____ .

4.   O →   To A for life, then to B for life, then to C for life.

A has a _____ ,

B has a _____ **in** _____ ,

C has a _____ **in** _____ ,

O has ? _____ .

5.   O →   To A for 10 years, then to B and the heirs of her body,
              then to C for life.

A has a_____,

B has a _____ **in** _____,

C has a _____ **in** _____,

O has ?_____.

6.   O →   To A for life, then to O and his heirs.

A has a_____,

O has a_____.

7.   O →   To A and the heirs of her body, then to B and the heirs
              of his body, then to C and her heirs, but if she begins
              to develop the property, then O has the right to re-enter
              and reclaim the property.

A has a_____,

B has a _____ **in** _____,

C has a _____ **in** _____,

O has ?_____.

8.   O →   To A for life, then to B and her heirs as long as she farms
              the land, then to C and her heirs.

A has a_____,

B has a _____ **in** _____,

C has a _____ **in** _____,

O has ?_____.

PROBLEM SET 5: REVIEW PROBLEMS

State the title to the following problems.

1.   O → A.

A has a_____,
O has ?_____.

2.   O → A and her heirs.

A has a_____,
O has ?_____ .[107]

3.   O → A for life.

4.   O → A and her heirs as long as the land is never used for commercial purposes.

5.   O → A and her heirs, but if the land is ever used for commercial purposes, then O and his heirs shall have the right to reenter and reclaim the land.

---

[107] The lines are here to remind you of the steps you should go through in analyzing the possessory estates and future interests. If you find this approach useful, you are encouraged to continue to use it, but the material will not provide the format any longer.

6.   O →   A and the heirs of her body.

7.   O →   A and her heirs as long as A uses the land for agricultural purposes, then to B and his heirs.

8.   O →   A and her heirs, but if A goes surfing, then to B and his heirs.

9.   O →   A and the heirs of her body, then to B and his heirs.

10.   O →   A and the heirs of her body, then if B is still living, to B and his heirs.

11.   O →   A and her children.

12.   O →   A for life, then to B and his heirs.

13.   O →   A for life, then to B and his heirs if B marries C, and if B does not, to D and his heirs.

14.   O →   A for life, then to B and his heirs if B returns from London.

15.   O →   A for life, then to the person who is then Dean of the Law
              School and his or her heirs.

16.   O →   A for life, then to B for life, then to C's heirs and their heirs.
              Assume C is still alive.

17.   O →   A for life, then to B and his heirs as long as the land is farmed.

18.   O →   A for life, then if B has agreed to farm the land, to B and his
              heirs.

19.   O →   A for life, then to B and his heirs if B marries C.

20.   O →   A for life, then to B and his heirs if B attends A's wedding.

Chapter 7

VARIATIONS ON THE EXECUTORY INTEREST

I. OVERVIEW

A. REVIEW

The analytical scheme developed so far is based upon three categories of possessory estates: the fee simple absolute, the fee simple defeasibles, and the finite estates. There are three fee simple defeasibles: the fee simple determinable, the fee simple subject to a condition subsequent, and a fee simple subject to an executory limitation.

B. HISTORICAL BACKGROUND

From a historical perspective, the fee simple subject to an executory limitation is "the new kid on the block." Pre-1536, if a fee simple were to be cut short, the future interest *had to be* in the grantor. Only the fee simple determinable ("To A and her heirs as long as she does not sell alcohol on the land") and the fee simple subject to condition subsequent ("To A and her heirs, but if she sells alcohol on the land, then O has the right to re-enter and reclaim the land") were permitted. Notice that both of these estates implicitly assume and require that the underlying fee simple defeasible is held by a third party.

In 1536, however, the Statute of Uses was adopted. The common law courts construed it as permitting a fee simple to be cut short with the future interest in a third party. To acknowledge this new combination, the courts gave the estates in the combination a new name: the fee simple subject to an executory limitation and the executory interest. The defining characteristic of this combination is that the future interest following a fee simple defeasible is held by a third party, not a grantor ("To A and her heirs, but if she sells alcohol on the land, to B and her heirs"). But inasmuch as the future interest is held by a third party, that opened up the possibility that the underlying fee simple defeasible could be held either by a third party *or the grantor*.

C. SHIFTING vs. SPRINGING EXECUTORY INTERESTS

The most common scenario is for a third party to hold the underlying fee simple defeasible. Under that scenario, the fee simple defeasible looks just like a fee simple determinable or a fee simple subject to a condition subsequent, except the future interest is held by a third party ("To A and her heirs as long as she farms the land, then to B and her heirs" or "To A and her heirs, but if she sells alcohol on the land, then to B and her heirs"). But because the future interest is held by a third party, the underlying fee simple defeasible is a fee simple subject to an executory limitation and the future interest held by third party is a **shifting** executory interest[108] (in fee simple).

Where, however, the underlying fee simple defeasible is *held by the grantor*, the future interest is called a **springing** executory interest. While the shifting executory interest is the more common executory interest, you need to be familiar with, and able to recognize, springing executory interests. Admittedly it is not as easy intuitively to envision a conveyance involving a springing executory interest. When springing executory interests do occur, they usually occur in one of two types of conveyances:[109] (1) the "future interest only" conveyance, or (2) the "gap" scenario conveyance.

II. SPRINGING EXECUTORY INTERESTS

A. THE "FUTURE INTEREST ONLY" CONVEYANCE

In all of the conveyances examined so far, the grantor has conveyed a possessory estate to the grantee (O → To A and her heirs). The moment the conveyance is effective, A holds the possessory estate.[110] But it is possible to draft a conveyance where the grantee takes a future interest, not a possessory estate. For example:

---

[108] Because the right to possession is being *shifted* from one third party to another.

[109] These scenarios were not permitted before the Statute of Uses was adopted in 1536. To reflect that these estate combinations are "new," the common law courts adopted new terminology to describe the estates.

[110] In fact, prior to 1536, for a conveyance to be valid, the grantee *had* to receive a possessory estate.

EXAMPLE 1

O →   To A and her heirs if A gets married.

Based on the wording of the conveyance, the logical assumption is that A is *not* married at the time of the conveyance. Assuming A is not married, A does not have the right to claim actual possession immediately after the conveyance. There is an express condition precedent which must be satisfied *before* A can claim the right to actual possession.

The presence of an express condition precedent which must be satisfied *before* the party's interest can become possessory makes the interest look a bit like, and sound a bit like, a *contingent* remainder. But here the interest cannot be a contingent remainder because it is not a remainder. There is no preceding finite estate. The express condition precedent is in the same clause as the clause which *appears* to be conveying a possessory interest to the grantee. It is not a possessory interest, however, due to the express condition precedent. The grantee is taking a future interest, not a possessory estate. The conveyance is a "**future interest only**" conveyance.

Because the grantee is taking a future interest only, the grantor retains the right to possession until the express condition precedent occurs – if it ever occurs. The assumption is that the grantor held a fee simple absolute before the conveyance. Where the conveyance is of a future interest only, the grantor's fee simple *may be* cut short if the express condition precedent occurs. Accordingly, after the conveyance, the grantor holds a fee simple defeasible. Because the future interest is held by a third party, the grantor must hold a fee simple subject to an executory limitation and the third party must hold an executory interest (in fee simple). Because the right to possession will be *taken from the grantor* if the possessory estate is cut short, the third party holds a *springing* executory interest in fee simple.

Anytime there is a "future interest only" conveyance (there is an express condition precedent that must be satisfied before the grantee has the right to claim actual possession under the conveyance), after the conveyance the grantor holds a fee simple subject to an executory limitation,[111] and the grantee holds a springing executory interest in fee simple.

---

[111] Assuming the grantor held a fee simple absolute before the conveyance.

B. THE "GAP" SCENARIO

The "gap" scenario arises when there is what appears to be a contingent remainder, but the express condition precedent is one which by its nature cannot be satisfied before the end of the preceding finite estate. For example:

EXAMPLE 2

O →   To A for life, then to B and her heirs if B marries A.

O →   To A for life, then to B and her heirs if B attends A's funeral.

State the title. In both conveyances A has a life estate. In both conveyances the express future interest is in B, a third party, so in both conveyances the future interest looks like a remainder. The words of limitation "and her heirs" in both conveyances indicate that the future interest is in fee simple. Is the future interest contingent or vested? In both conveyances the future interest looks like a contingent remainder because there is an express condition precedent in the same clause as the clause creating the future interest which must be satisfied before the interest can become possessory.   In both conveyances the future interest looks like a contingent remainder.

But upon closer inspection of the express condition precedent in the respective conveyances, it becomes apparent that there is a difference. In the first conveyance ("To A for life, then to B and her heirs if B marries A"), the express condition precedent is one which by its nature is capable of occurring (being satisfied) during or at the moment the preceding finite estate ends. B will either marry A or not during A's life estate. Because the express condition precedent has a chance of occurring during the preceding finite estate, the future interest is a contingent remainder.

In the second conveyance ("To A for life, then to B and her heirs if B attends A's funeral"), however, the express condition precedent is one which by its nature *cannot* be fulfilled during the preceding finite estate. Temporally there is a "gap" between the end of the preceding finite estate and the point in time when the express condition precedent could occur.   The express condition precedent is that B must attend A's funeral. B cannot attend A's funeral until *after* A dies. The express condition precedent cannot be satisfied before, or at the moment, the preceding finite estate ends; the express condition precedent is such that it cannot be satisfied until *after* the preceding finite estate ends. There is, implicitly, a temporal "gap" between the end of the finite estate and the point in time when the express condition precedent may be satisfied.

Because the conveyance did not expressly provide for who had the right to possession at that point in time, by default the grantor held the future interest following the finite estate – the grantor held a reversion in fee simple. That meant that the express clause granting the future interest to the third party if the condition were to occur would have to cut short the grantor's fee simple with the future interest in a third party. Pre-1536, if a fee simple were to be cut short, the future interest **had to be** in the grantor. Thus, pre-1536, the future interest following the "gap" type conveyance was null and void.

Post-1536, however, the "gap" type conveyance is just a variation on the fee simple subject to an executory limitation with a *springing* executory interest combination. In the "gap" type conveyance, the grantor's reversion in fee simple might be cut short by the express condition precedent which could not, by nature, occur during the preceding finite estate. Inasmuch as the grantor's reversion in fee simple might be cut short, the grantor holds a fee simple defeasible. In the "gap" scenario, the future interest will always be held by a third party. The grantor then holds a fee simple subject to an executory limitation and the third party holds a springing executory interest (in fee simple).

The "gap" scenario is fairly easy to identify as long as the conveyance is read carefully. Watch for a conveyance which appears to create a contingent remainder because of the presence of an express condition precedent, except the express condition precedent, by nature, cannot be fulfilled during the preceding finite estate. Whenever that is the case, there is a "gap" scenario. Whenever there is a "gap" scenario, the grantor will hold a reversion in fee simple subject to an executory limitation to cover the gap, and the third party will hold an executory interest in fee simple. Because the executory interest, if it is to become possessory, will take the right to possession from the grantor and give it to a third party, it is a *springing* executory interest in fee simple.[112]

---

[112] The preceding finite estate is almost always a life estate, but in theory it can be

III. THE VESTED REMAINDER SUBJECT TO DIVESTMENT

The common law courts also construed the Statute of Uses as permitting another "new" conveyance – one in which a party who held a vested remainder could *lose* the right to possession *before* he or she ever took possession of the property. Again, the statement is so abstract a couple of examples should help:

EXAMPLE 3

O → To A for life, then to B and her heirs, but if B stops farming the land, then to C and her heirs.

O → To A for life, then to B and her heirs, but if A stops farming the land, then to C and her heirs.

State the titles. In both conveyances, A has a life estate. In both conveyances, because the future interest is in B, B holds a remainder. In both conveyances, the words of limitation "and her heirs" indicate that B's interest is in fee simple. Moreover, in both conveyances B's remainder is vested. The party holding the remainder, B, is born, ascertainable, and reading comma to comma, there is no express condition precedent in the same clause creating the remainder or the preceding clause. But in both conveyances the fee simple is not a fee simple absolute because there is additional language which qualifies B's fee simple. At first blush, it would appear that B has a fee simple defeasible – a fee simple which might be cut short by an express condition precedent.

That is the case in the first conveyance, but not in the second. In the first conveyance ("To A for life, then to B and her heirs, but if B stops farming the land, then to C and her heirs"), the express condition that may terminate B's interest is "if **B** stops farming the land ... ." That condition applies to and qualifies B's right to possession *after* B takes actual possession. It is an express condition subsequent. B holds a vested remainder in fee

---

any of the finite estates. It is difficult to imagine, however, a "gap" scenario where the preceding finite estate is a fee tail. The norm is for the preceding finite estate to be a life estate, though occasionally it will be a term of years.

simple subject to an executory limitation, and C holds a shifting executory interest in fee simple.

But in the second conveyance ("To A for life, then to B and her heirs, but if A stops farming the land, then to C and her heirs"), the express condition that may terminate B's interest is "if **A** stops farming the land, ..." Relative to B's interest, that event must occur, if at all, *during* A's life estate – *before* B's interest becomes possessory. It is an express condition precedent relative to B's future interest becoming possessory. It is not an express condition precedent which must be satisfied before B's interest can become possessory, rather it is an express condition precedent which, if it occurs, will shift the right to possession from A to C, thereby destroying (or "divesting") B's vested remainder.

Pre-1536, once a vested remainder vested, the right to possession could not be taken away from the party before it became possessory. But after the Statute of Uses in 1536, the common law courts construed the statute as permitting the right to possession under a vested remainder to be taken away before it became possessory. Because this was a "new" combination of estates, the courts again created new terminology to acknowledge this "new" development. The vested remainder is said to be "subject to divestment" and the future interest following a vested remainder subject to divestment is an "executory interest."[113]

Returning to the second conveyance above, the title is that A has a life estate, B holds a vested remainder in fee simple subject to divestment, and C holds an executory interest in fee simple. Which type of executory interest, springing or shifting? Because the right to possession would be taken from one third party and "shifted" to another third party if the condition were to occur, C's executory interest is a shifting executory interest.

Notice, in analyzing any **remainder** which has an express condition qualifying it, there are two key variables. First, is the express condition a condition precedent or a condition subsequent? If a condition subsequent, and the remainder is in fee simple, the estate is one of the fee simple defeasibles. Second, if the express condition is a condition precedent, the key is where in

---

[113] Notice the term "executory interest" is used to describe the future interest in all the "new" estate combinations permitted after the Statute of Uses; and all of them are held by a third party. You should never use the term "executory interest" to describe a future interest held by the grantor.

the conveyance is the condition expressed? If the condition precedent is in the same clause as the clause creating the remainder, or the preceding clause, the remainder is a contingent remainder. If the condition precedent is in a clause subsequent to the clause creating the remainder, the remainder is a vested remainder subject to divestment, and the future interest following it will be a shifting executory interest in fee simple.

Although vested remainders subject to divestment look rather straightforward in isolation, when contrasted with other conveyances some students have difficultly distinguishing them. It might help you identify the vested remainder subject to divestment if you pay close attention to several requirements which are implicit in the analysis of the vested remainder subject to divestment.

A. THE REQUIREMENT OF A VESTED REMAINDER

Before there can be a vested remainder subject to divestment, there must be a vested remainder. There is no chance that an estate is a vested remainder subject to divestment unless (1) there is a remainder, and (2) it is a vested remainder. That means that the preceding estate in the conveyance must be a finite possessory estate (typically a life estate). If there is no preceding finite possessory estate, the express condition cannot be one which could occur *before* the party takes possession. For example:

EXAMPLE 4

O →   To B and her heirs, but if B sells alcohol on the land, then to C and her heirs.

O →   To A for life, then to B and her heirs, but if A sells alcohol on the land, then to C and her heirs.

Notice in the first conveyance, there is no finite estate. The qualifying condition which could affect the party's right to possession ("if B sells alcohol on the land …") is a condition subsequent. B holds a fee simple defeasible. Because the future interest is held by C, a third party, B holds a fee simple subject to an executory limitation, and C holds a shifting executory interest in fee simple. In contrast, in the second conveyance, there is a preceding finite estate. A holds a life estate, B holds a vested remainder, and the express condition is a condition precedent – it must occur, if at all, during the finite estate preceding the vested remainder ("if A sells alcohol on the land ..."). Because the condition is one which must occur, if at all, prior to B's remainder becoming possessory, the remainder is a vested remainder subject to divestment.

B. THE EXPRESS CONDITION PRECEDENT REQUIREMENT

Another point which is implicit in the discussion of the vested remainder subject to divestment is that the condition must be an express condition **precedent** – not a condition subsequent. For example:

EXAMPLE 5

O → To A and her heirs as long as she maintains the wetlands on the property.

O → To A and her heirs, but if she fails to maintain the wetlands on the property, then O has the right to re-enter and reclaim the property.

O → To A and her heirs as long as she maintains the wetlands on the property, then to B and her heirs.

O → To A and her heirs, but if she fails to maintain the wetlands on the property, then to B and her heirs.

O → To A for life, then to B and her heirs as long as she maintains the wetlands on the property, then to C and her heirs.

O → To A for life, then to B and her heirs, but if B fails to maintain the wetlands on the property, then to C and her heirs.

In all of the conveyances the express condition is a condition subsequent. In the first four conveyances, there is no preceding finite estate, so the possessory estate is one of the fee simple defeasibles. In the last two, there is a preceding finite estate, but the express condition qualifying the remainder is still a condition subsequent (applies subsequent to the remainder becoming possessory), so the remainder in each of the last two conveyances is a vested remainder in fee simple defeasible, not subject to divestment.

There must be a vested remainder and an express condition **precedent** in the clause subsequent to the remainder before the remainder can be a vested remainder subject to divestment.

EXAMPLE 6

O →   To A for life, then to B and her heirs, but if B fails to maintain the wetlands on the property, then to C and her heirs.

O →   To A for life, then to B and her heirs, but if A fails to maintain the wetlands on the property, then to C and her heirs.

In the first conveyance there is a vested remainder, but the express condition qualifying it ("but if B fails to maintain the wetlands ...") is a condition subsequent. The express condition is one which by its nature must occur, if at all, only after B's remainder becomes possessory. B holds a vested remainder in fee simple subject to an executory limitation. In the second conveyance there is a vested remainder, and the express condition qualifying it ("but if A fails to maintain the wetlands ...") is a condition precedent. The express condition is one which by its nature must occur, if at all, only *before* B's remainder becomes possessory. It must occur, if at all, during the preceding finite estate. Because B's vested remainder is qualified by an express condition precedent in the clause subsequent to the clause creating the remainder, B holds a vested remainder in fee simple subject to divestment, and C holds a shifting executory interest in fee simple.

The next point which is implicit in the analysis of vested remainders is a relatively minor point - the condition precedent must be express. The "subject to divestment" component of the analysis must be the result of an express condition in the conveyance, not because of the nature of the remainder. For example:

EXAMPLE 7

O →   To A for life, then to B for life, then to C and her heirs.

O →   To A for life, then to B and her heirs, but if B dies before A, then to C and her heirs.

State the title. In the first conveyance, A has a life estate, B has a vested remainder in life estate, and C has a vested remainder in fee simple. But if B dies before A, B will lose her right to possession before B's remainder becomes possessory. Does that mean that the remainder is subject to divestment? No. That is the nature of a life estate – it is not an express condition precedent. The vested remainder is subject to divestment only if there is an express condition in the subsequent clause which could occur prior to the vested remainder becoming possessory. In the second conveyance, B's death before A's death is the express condition precedent. The state of the title is A holds a life estate, B holds a vested remainder in fee simple subject to divestment, and C holds a shifting executory interest in fee simple.

C. THE CONDITION PRECEDENT MUST BE IN THE CLAUSE SUBSEQUENT

Related to the points made above is that the express condition precedent must be in the clause ***subsequent*** to the clause creating the remainder. If the express condition precedent is in the same clause as the clause creating the remainder or the preceding clause, then the condition precedent makes the remainder a contingent remainder. Where there is an express condition precedent, the remainder will either be a contingent remainder or a vested remainder subject to divestment – there will not be a contingent remainder subject to divestment.

EXAMPLE 8

O →   To A for life, then if A restores the wetlands on the property, to B and her heirs.

O →   To A for life, then to B and her heirs if A restores the wetlands on the property.

O →   To A for life, then to B and her heirs, but if A fails to restore the wetlands on the property, then to C and her heirs.

O →   To A for life, then if A restores the wetlands on the property, to B and her heirs, but if A fails to restore the wetlands on the property, then to C and her heirs.

In all four conveyances, A holds a life estate, and because B holds the future interest, B holds a remainder in fee simple. In all four conveyances, B's remainder is qualified by an express condition precedent relating to A restoring the wetlands on the property. In the first two conveyances, the express condition precedent is in the same clause creating B's remainder or the preceding clause, so B's remainder is a contingent remainder is fee simple. There is no express taker in the event the express condition precedent is not satisfied, so O, the grantor, holds a default reversion in fee simple.

In the third conveyance, A holds a life estate, B holds a remainder in fee simple, and the express condition precedent is in the clause after the clause creating B's remainder. B's remainder is a vested remainder in fee simple subject to divestment, and C holds a shifting executory interest in fee simple. The location of the express condition precedent in the conveyance is critical to the analysis.

In the fourth conveyance, A holds a life estate and B holds a remainder in fee simple. Because the express condition precedent is in the same clause as the clause creating the remainder, B holds a contingent remainder in fee simple. But what about the clause which goes on to re-state the express condition precedent in the clause subsequent to the clause creating the remainder? That is just re-stating the express condition precedent which also qualifies C's interest. This is just another example of alternative contingent remainders. B holds a contingent remainder in fee simple, and C holds an alternative contingent remainder in fee simple – contingent on A failing to maintain the wetlands. B's *contingent* remainder is *not subject to divestment*. B holds a contingent remainder in fee simple, and C holds an alternative contingent remainder in fee simple. There must be a vested remainder before there can be a vested remainder subject to divestment. To complete the state of the title, O, the grantor, holds a default reversion in fee simple (in the event the preceding finite estate ends prematurely and the first contingent remainder has not vested).

D. EXPRESS CONDITION WHICH CAN BE EITHER PRECEDENT OR SUBSEQUENT

The material so far has discussed the express condition precedent and the express condition subsequent separately, thereby creating the impression that the same condition could not be both. It is possible, however, to have an express condition that could be both – a condition which could occur before the remainder becomes possessory and which could also occur after the remainder becomes possessory. This is particularly true where the express condition is not tied to the use of the land or the life of the party holding the preceding finite estate. For example:

EXAMPLE 9

O → To A for life, then to B and her heirs, but if A sells alcohol on the property, then to C and her heirs.

O → To A for life, then to B and her heirs, but if B sells alcohol on the property, to C and her heirs.

O → To A for life, then to B and her heirs, but if A marries C, then to C and her heirs.

O → To A for life, then to B and her heirs, but if X marries Y, then to C and her heirs.

In all four conveyances, A holds a life estate. In all four conveyances, because a third party holds the future interest, B holds a remainder. In all four conveyances, because B is born, ascertainable, and there is no express condition in the clause creating the remainder or the preceding clause, B holds a vested remainder (in fee simple because of the express words of limitation "and her heirs"). But there is express language qualifying B's remainder in all four conveyances in the clause after the clause creating the remainder. What type of vested remainder in fee simple does B hold in each?

In the first conveyance, the condition is an express condition precedent which must occur, if at all, during the preceding finite estate (either A will or will not sell alcohol on the land during A's lifetime). B holds a vested remainder in fee simple subject to divestment, and C holds a shifting executory interest in fee simple.

In the second conveyance, the condition is an express condition subsequent which must occur, it at all, during the time that the remainder is possessory (either B will or will not sell alcohol on the land *after* B takes possession of the land).[114] Because the condition is a condition subsequent, B holds a vested remainder in fee simple subject to an executory limitation, and C holds a shifting executory interest in fee simple.

In the third conveyance, the condition is one which is not tied to the land, rather it is tied to the life tenant, and because it is tied to the preceding life tenant, it must occur, if at all, during the preceding finite estate. Either A will get married or not during A's lifetime. The express condition "if A marries C" is an express condition precedent relative to B's remainder. B holds a vested remainder in fee simple subject to divestment, and C holds a shifting executory interest in fee simple.

In the fourth conveyance, the express condition is not tied to the property or to the life tenant. The express condition is one which could occur before the remainder becomes possessory – but it could still occur after the remainder becomes possessory. As long as the condition is one which could occur before the remainder becomes possessory, the remainder is a vested remainder subject to divestment. At the time of the conveyance, and up until the remainder becomes possessory, B's vested remainder in fee simple is subject to divestment. If the preceding finite estate ends, and the express condition has not occurred yet but such that it could still occur, the remainder becomes the possessory estate – but the estate could still be cut short if the

---

[114] Assume that B does not have access to the land during the preceding finite estate. That is the norm and the logical assumption.

condition were to occur. For example, in the fourth conveyance above, assume that the facts went on to tell you that A died. B's remainder becomes possessory the moment the finite estate ends, so it no longer is a remainder. B holds the property in fee simple. But because the express condition could still occur even after B takes possession (X could still marry Y), B's fee simple could be cut short. The express condition is only a condition subsequent now. B holds a fee simple defeasible. If B's right to possession were cut short, the right to possession would go to C – a third party. That means that B would hold a fee simple subject to an executory limitation, and C would hold a shifting executory interest in fee simple.[115] The analysis of possessory estates and future interests can change over time.

E. EFFECT UPON THE PRECEDING FINITE ESTATE

One final point about divesting conditions is that there is almost always an inherent ambiguity with respect to what effect, if any, the divesting condition should have upon the preceding finite estate. If the divesting condition occurs during the course of the preceding finite estate, does it only divest the vested remainder or should it also cut short the preceding finite estate (i.e., immediately terminate the preceding finite estate)? For example:

EXAMPLE 10

O →   To A for life, then to B and her heirs, but if A fails to graduates from law school, then to C and her heirs.

State the title. A has a life estate, B has a vested remainder in fee simple subject to divestment, and C has a shifting executory interest in fee simple. Assume that the facts go on to state that A dies without having graduated from law school. The divesting condition has occurred, and B's vested remainder in fee simple is divested. B loses her right to possession before it ever becomes possessory. Notice that the nature of the divesting condition is such

---

[115] Technically one could argue that before B's vested remainder became possessory the proper state of the title should have been that B held a vested remainder, subject to divestment, in fee simple, subject to an executory limitation. This accurately reflects that B's remainder is, at that point in time, subject to both (1) the possibility of divestment before becoming possessory, and (2) subject to being cut short after becoming possessory. This level of detail, however, is usually more than is necessary in the introductory coverage.

that it is not tested until the end of the preceding finite estate, so by its nature, it has no effect upon the preceding finite estate.

Often, however, the express divesting condition is one which may occur during the preceding finite estate, and if it does, a question which may arise is whether the divesting condition should also cut short the preceding finite estate. For example:

EXAMPLE 11

O → To A for life, then to B and her heirs, but if A marries X, then to C and her heirs.

State the title. A has a life estate, B has a vested remainder in fee simple subject to divestment, and C has a shifting executory interest in fee simple. Now assume the problem goes on to state that after the conveyance, A marries X. How does A's marriage to X affect the state of the title?

A marrying X constitutes the divesting condition, so at a minimum B's vested remainder in fee simple is divested. B lost her right to possession before it ever became possessory. But has A also lost her right to possession? Should the divesting condition be construed not only to divest the remainder, but also to cut short the preceding finite estate?

Ultimately that is a question of the grantor's intent. There is an inherent ambiguity in the phrasing of the conveyance. Does the word "then" in the clause "then to C and her heirs" describe the moment the divesting condition occurs or the moment the preceding finite estate ends? If the grantor intended the word "then" to refer to the moment the divesting condition occurred, then the divesting condition would also cut short the preceding finite estate. If that is the intended effect, that intent needs to be reflected in the state of the title. The phrase "subject to an executory limitation" should be added to the name of the preceding finite estate. With respect to the example above, if the grantor intended that if A married X that event would not only divest B's vested remainder but also cut short A's life estate, the proper state of the title would be: A holds a life estate subject to an executory limitation, B holds a vested remainder subject to divestment, and C holds a shifting executory limitation in fee simple.

Whether the divesting condition should be construed as only divesting the vested remainder or whether it should be construed as also cutting short the preceding finite estate is beyond the scope of this introductory coverage. It would require a subtle analysis of the grantor's intent based on the nature of the condition and the express words used that would require more time than it is worth in the introductory coverage. The material will assume that the divesting condition only divested the vested remainder and does not affect the underlying finite estate. In answering the problems in this book, assume that the divesting condition never cuts short the preceding finite estate. If your professor decides to cover this issue, listen carefully to him or her for guidance as to when the language of the conveyance should be construed as not only divesting the remainder but also cutting short the finite estate.

IV. RECAP

The most common executory interest is the shifting executory interest following a fee simple subject to an executory limitation. But it is also possible to have a springing executory interest (the "future interest only" conveyance or the "gap" scenario) following a fee simple subject to an executory limitation; and where a vested remainder has an express condition precedent in the clause subsequent to the clause creating the remainder, the vested remainder is subject to divestment and the future interest is a shifting executory interest in fee simple.

When there is a vested remainder in fee simple, followed by an express qualifying condition and the future interest is in a third party, the key is **when** the qualifying condition may occur. If the qualifying condition **may occur prior** to the vested remainder becoming possessory, the vested remainder is subject to divestment and the future interest in the third party is a shifting executory interest in fee simple. If the qualifying condition **can occur only after** the vested remainder has become possessory, the remainder is a vested remainder in fee simple subject to an executory limitation, and the future interest is a shifting executory interest in fee simple.

PROBLEM SET 6

1.   O →   To A for life, then to B and her heirs as long as the land is
           farmed.

2.   O →   To A for life, then to B and her heirs, but if B stops farming the
           land, then O can re-enter and reclaim the land.

3.   O →   To A for life, then to B and her heirs as long as the land is
           farmed, then to C and her heirs.

4.   O →   To A for life, then to B and her heirs, but if B stops farming the
           land, then to C and her heirs.

5.   O →   To A for life, then to B and her heirs, then to C and her heirs.

6.   O →   To A for life, then to B and her heirs, but if B sells alcohol on the land, then to X and her heirs.

         (a)   Assume A, B and X are alive.

         (b)   Assume A dies and B and X are alive.

7.   O →   To A for life, then to B and her heirs if B graduates from law school.

         Assume A and B are both alive and B has not graduated from law school yet.

8.   O →   To A and her heirs if A graduates from medical school.

PROBLEM SET 7

1.   O →   To A for life, then to B and her heirs as long as the land is farmed.

2.   O →   To A for life, then to B and her heirs, but if B stops farming the land, then O can re-enter and reclaim the land.

3.   O →   To A for life, then to B and her heirs as long as the land is farmed, then to C and her heirs.

4.   O →   To A for life, then to B and her heirs, but if B stops farming the land, then to C and her heirs.

5.   O →   To A for life, then to B and her heirs, but if A stops farming the land, then to C and her heirs.

6.   O →   To A for life, then to B and her heirs, but if B marries C, then to X and her heirs.

(a) Assume A, B, C and X are alive.

(b) Assume A dies and B, C and X are alive.

7. O → To A for life, then to B and her heirs if B graduates from law school.

    Assume A and B are both alive and B has not graduated from law school yet.

8. O → To A for life, then to B and her heirs, but if A fails to graduate from law school, then to C and her heirs.

9. O → To A for life, then to B and her heirs if A graduates from law school, but if A fails to graduate from law school, then to C and her heirs.

10. O → To A for life, then to B and her heirs as long as B farms the land.

11. O → To A for life, then to B and her heirs, but if C returns from England, then to C and her heirs.

Chapter 8

DISTINGUISHING THE CONDITION PRECEDENT FROM THE CONDITION SUBSEQUENT FROM THE DIVESTING CONDITION

I. OVERVIEW

Presented individually, the basic scheme of possessory estates and future interests does not look that intimidating or difficult. But when presented with a batch of problems mixing the different estates into different combinations, many students fall into the Bermuda Triangle of possessory estates and future interests. They have difficulty distinguishing a condition precedent from a condition subsequent from a divesting condition, and thus confuse contingent remainders, vested remainders subject to divestment, and fee simple defeasibles. The material will start with the basic and move to the more complicated.

II. REVISITING THE CONDITION SUBSEQUENT

The first condition the material presented, and in many respects the easiest to understand and recognize, was the condition subsequent. A condition subsequent is a condition which affects a grantee's **right to retain possession** of the property *after* the grantee has taken possession. The condition subsequent is the defining characteristic of the fee simple defeasibles: the fee simple determinable, the fee simple subject to a condition subsequent, and the fee simple subject to an executory limitation. The only difference between (1) the fee simple determinable, the fee simple subject to a condition subsequent, and (2) the fee simple subject to an executory limitation, is who holds the future interest following the estate: the grantor (the first two estates) or a third party (in which case the estate is a fee simple subject to an executory limitation). The only difference between the fee simple determinable and the fee simple subject to a condition subsequent is whether the condition subsequent automatically terminates the estate (in which case it is a fee simple determinable) or whether the condition subsequent gives the grantor the right to re-enter and terminate the estate (in which case it is a fee simple subject to a condition subsequent).

The differences and similarities among the three condition subsequent estates are evident in the following conveyances:

EXAMPLE 1

O → To A and her heirs as long as she does not sell alcohol on the land.

O → To A and her heirs, but if she sells alcohol on the land, O has the right to re-enter and re-claim the land.

O → To A and her heirs as long as she does not sell alcohol on the land, then to B and her heirs.

O → To A and her heirs, but if she sells alcohol on the land, then to B and her heirs.

The first conveyance is a classic example of a fee simple determinable. The second conveyance is a classic example of a fee simple subject to a condition subsequent. The third and fourth conveyances are classic examples of a fee simple subject to an executory limitation. In all four conveyances, the condition concerning the sale of alcohol is a condition subsequent in that it affects A's (the grantee's) **right to *retain* possession** of the property *after* A has taken possession of the property. The words of limitation typically[116] introducing a condition subsequent are "**as long as/so long as** ..." and "**but if/however/provided that** ... **.**" In all four conveyances, reading comma to comma, the condition subsequent is either in the same clause creating the estate or in the immediately subsequent clause.

---

[116] Be particularly careful to note that these observations are *generally* true but cannot be taken as hard and fast absolute rules.

III. REVISITING THE CONDITION PRECEDENT

A. REVISITING CONTINGENT REMAINDERS

The second condition analyzed, and one which is also fairly easy to understand and recognize, is the condition precedent. A condition precedent is a condition which affects a grantee's **right to** *take* **possession** of the property *before* the grantee has taken possession of the property. The condition precedent is the defining characteristic of the contingent remainder.

EXAMPLE 2

O → To A for life, then to B and her heirs if she graduates from law school.

O → To A for life, then if B graduates from law school, to B and her heirs.

Both of these conveyances are classic examples of contingent remainders. In both of these conveyances, the condition concerning B graduating from law school is a condition precedent in that it affects B's (the grantee's) **right to** *take* **possession** of the property *before* B has taken possession of the property. It is a condition which must be satisfied *before* the grantee can take possession of the property. The words of limitation typically[117] introducing a condition precedent *for purposes of the contingent remainder* is simply "**if** ... ." Reading comma to comma, the condition precedent introducing a contingent remainder is either in the same clause creating the estate or in the immediately preceding clause.

B. REVISITING THE DIVESTING CONDITION

The divesting condition is where the water suddenly turns murky. The reason is that the divesting condition looks a lot like *both* of the other conditions. For example:

---

[117] Be particularly careful to note that these observations are *generally* true but cannot be taken as hard and fast absolute rules.

EXAMPLE 3

O → To A for life, then to B and her heirs, but if A fails to graduate from law school, then to C and her heirs.

This conveyance is a classic example of a vested remainder subject to divestment. The divesting condition is a condition precedent: B's right to take possession is dependent upon whether A graduates from law school, an event which must occur (or not occur, as the case may be) during the A's life estate. If A fails to graduate from law school, B's vested right to take possession of the property will be divested. The divesting condition is a condition precedent because it affects the grantee's right to take possession of the property *before* the grantee, has taken possession of the property.

That, however, appears to be the same definition used to define the condition precedent for purposes of a contingent remainder. What is the difference? The difference is in the wording and structure of the conveyance. In the contingent remainder, the condition precedent is in the *same* clause creating the remainder or the *preceding* clause and is typically[118] introduced by the word "*if* ...." In contrast, in the vested remainder subject to divestment, the condition precedent is in the clause *immediately following* the clause creating the remainder and is typically introduced by the words "***but if... .***"

EXAMPLE 4

O → To A for life, then to B and her heirs if A graduates from law school.

O → To A for life, then if A graduates from law school, to B and her heirs.

O → To A for life, then to B and her heirs, but if A fails to graduate from law school, then to C and her heirs.

---

[118] Be particularly careful to note that these observations are *generally* true but cannot be taken as hard and fast absolute rules.

In all three of the above conveyances, the condition precedent to B taking possession of the property is that A must graduate from law school. The key is in which clause the condition is expressed. In the first two conveyances – the contingent remainder conveyances – the condition precedent is either in the same clause creating the remainder or the preceding clause and it is introduced by the word "if ...." In the third conveyance – the conveyance creating the vested remainder subject to divestment – the condition precedent is in clause subsequent to the clause creating the remainder and the condition precedent is introduced by the words "but if ...."

Notice the potential confusion that can arise if you automatically assume too much about the use of the words "but if ..." to introduce the express condition. The phrase *"but if ..."* are the words of limitation which typically introduce the *condition subsequent* in the fee simple subject to a condition subsequent and the fee simple subject to an executory limitation. But the phrase *"but if ... "* can also introduce a *condition precedent* for purposes of the vested remainder subject to divestment. That is one of the reasons why the divesting condition is sometimes confused by students with the condition subsequent. Return to the first set of conveyances:

EXAMPLE 5

O → To A and her heirs as long as she does not sell alcohol on the land.

O → To A and her heirs, but if she sells alcohol on the land, O shall have the right to re-enter and re-claim the land.

O → To A and her heirs as long as she does not sell alcohol on the land, then to B and her heirs.

O → To A and her heirs, but if she sells alcohol on the land, then to B and her heirs.

It is unlikely that anyone would mistake these conveyances for a vested remainder subject to divestment because there is no vested remainder in any of the conveyances. While that is true, it is easy to throw a life estate at the front to show the difficulty distinguishing (1) the vested remainder subject to a condition subsequent and the vested remainder subject to an executory limitation from (2) the vested remainder subject to divestment.

EXAMPLE 6

O → To A for life, then to B and her heirs, but if B sells alcohol on the land, then O has the right to re-enter and re-claim the property.

O → To A for life, then to B and her heirs, but if B sells alcohol on the land, then to C and her heirs.

O → To A for life, then to B and her heirs, but if A sells alcohol on the land, then to C and her heirs.

In all three of the conveyances, the words of limitation introducing the condition is the phrase "but if ... ." Obviously no hard and fast rule about the characterization of an estate can be derived simply from the use of that phrase. The vested remainder subject to a condition subsequent is somewhat easy to identify because of the express clause giving O, the grantor, the right to re-enter and re-claim the property following the occurrence of the condition subsequent. But distinguishing the vested remainder subject to an executory limitation from the vested remainder subject to divestment is much more difficult and much more subtle.

C. ANALYTICAL KEYS

The key to distinguishing the vested remainder subject to an executory limitation from the vested remainder subject to divestment is *when* the condition may occur: if the condition may occur *before* the remainder becomes possessory, the estate is *a vested remainder subject to divestment; if* the condition may occur only *after* the remainder becomes possessory, the estate is *a vested remainder subject to an executory limitation.* Looking at the second and third conveyances, there is only one difference in the express wording of the conveyances. In the second conveyance, the condition must occur, if at all, while B has possession of the property. Because the condition can only occur, if at all, after B's remainder becomes possessory, the condition is a condition subsequent – and thus the estate is a vested remainder subject to an executory limitation. In contrast, in the third conveyance, the condition must occur, if at all, while A has possession of the property. Because the condition can only occur, if at all, before B's remainder becomes possessory, the condition is a condition precedent and hence the estate is a vested remainder subject to divestment.

What if the condition is one which may occur before *or* after the remainder becomes possessory? For example:

EXAMPLE 7

O →   To A for life, then to B and her heirs, but if C graduates from law school, then to C and her heirs.

First of all, in stating the title you should be able to narrow the choices concerning which estate B has. A has a life estate, so B's interest must be a remainder. Is it a vested remainder or a contingent remainder? Is the condition: (1) in the same clause creating the remainder or the preceding clause, or (2) in the immediately following clause? The latter, so it is not a contingent remainder but rather a vested remainder. Is it a vested remainder: (1) in fee simple absolute; (2) in one of the fee simple defeasible; (3) in fee simple subject to an executory limitation; or (4) in fee simple subject to divestment? Because there is additional qualifying language, and the future interest is in a third party, the vested remainder cannot be in fee simple absolute or in one of the fee simple defeasible (a fee simple determinable or a fee simple subject to a condition subsequent). It has to be either a vested remainder subject to an executory limitation or a vested remainder subject to divestment.

The key is whether the condition is one which *may* occur prior to the remainder becoming possessory. Is it conceivable that C could graduate from law school while A is still alive? Certainly. Therefore, while A is still alive, B holds a vested remainder subject to divestment. But what if the facts told you that thereafter A died, but B and C were still alive. State the title. Following these factual developments, the conveyance in essence would read as follows:

EXAMPLE 8

O → To B and her heirs, but if C graduates from law school, then to C and her heirs.

B's interest has become possessory, so it is no longer a remainder, but it is still subject to the possibility that C may graduate from law school. But now that condition can only occur, if at all, after the estate which was the remainder has become possessory. B would hold a fee simple subject to an executory limitation, and C would hold a shifting executory interest in fee simple. To distinguish the vested remainder in fee simple subject to an executory limitation from a vested remainder in fee simple subject to divestment, the key is the express condition and whether it is a condition subsequent or a condition precedent.

As if that were not enough murkiness, the "but if ..." words can also appear in the express words of a contingent remainder, thus completing the Bermuda triangle.

EXAMPLE 9

O → To A for life, then to B and her heirs, **but if** A sells alcohol on the land, then to C and her heirs.

O → To A for life, then to B and her heirs, **but if** B sells alcohol on the land, then to C and her heirs.

O → To A for life, then if B agrees in writing not to sell alcohol on the land, to B and her heirs, but if B refuses to agree not to sell alcohol on the land, then to C and her heirs.

The key to analyzing these complex conveyances is to read comma to comma, clause to clause. In the first two conveyances, the second clause creates a vested remainder in B in fee simple of some sort, and because the future interest is in a third party, the only question is whether the vested remainder is a vested remainder subject to an executory limitation or a vested remainder subject to divestment.   As discussed in the prior paragraph, the focus is on whether the condition can occur before or after the remainder becomes possessory: if before, the vested remainder is subject to divestment; if after, the vested remainder is subject to a limitation.

In the third and final conveyance, reading comma to comma, reading the second clause we find an express condition precedent introduced by the word "if ... ."   Thus the remainder is a contingent remainder.   But what about the "but if ..." clause?   It simply states the opposite of the condition precedent and thus serves to introduce the alternative contingent remainder.   You can always spot when the "but if ..." phrase is being used to introduce an alternative contingent remainder because (1) it will immediately follow a clause creating a contingent remainder, and (2) you can strike the whole "but if ..." clause and simply insert the word "otherwise, ..." As you should have discerned by now, do not put too much weight on the introductory words "but if ... ." In and of themselves, they do not help you very much in analyzing which estate a conveyance creates.

Having now navigated through the potentially choppy and murky waters of the Bermuda Triangle of possessory estate and future interests, you should be in store for some smooth sailing (at least until the Rule against Perpetuities!).

IV.   RECAP

The distinguishing characteristic of the *fee simple defeasibles* (the fee simple determinable, the fee simple subject to a condition subsequent, and the fee simple subject to an executory limitation) is that there is a *condition subsequent* which affects the grantee's right to retain possession of the property *after* the grantee has taken possession of the property.   The distinguishing characteristic of the *contingent remainder* is that there is a *condition precedent* which affects the grantee's right to take possession of the property *before* the grantee has taken possession of the property.   The distinguishing characteristic of the *vested remainder subject to divestment* is that the grantee's right to take possession is subject to a *condition precedent* which is expressed in the *clause immediately following* the clause creating the remainder.   In distinguishing the vested remainder subject to an executory limitation and the vested remainder subject to divestment, the key is whether the qualifying condition expressed in the clause immediately following the clause creating the remainder is one which *may occur before* the remainder becomes possessory (in which case the remainder is a vested remainder subject to divestment) or if the condition is *one which can only occur, if at all, after* the remainder becomes possessory (in which case the remainder is a vested remainder subject to an executory limitation).

PROBLEM SET 8

State the title to the following conveyances.

1.   O →   To A for life, then to B and her heirs if B attends A's funeral.

2.   O →   To A for life, then to B and her heirs if B graduates from law school.

       Assume A has died and B has not graduated from law school yet.

3.   O →   To A and her heirs as long as the land is farmed, then to B and her heirs.

4.   O →   To A and her heirs, but if the land is used for commercial purposes, then to B and her heirs.

5.   O →   To A and her heirs if she graduates from law school.

6.   O →   To A for life, then after A's funeral, to B and her heirs.

7.   O →   To A for life, then to B and his heirs, but if B and his heirs ever use the land for commercial purposes, then to C and her heirs.

8.   O →   To A for life, then to B and his heirs, but if A and her heirs ever use the land for commercial purposes, then to C and her heirs.

ONE LAST SET OF ESTATES: LIFE ESTATE DEFEASIBLES

I. OVERVIEW

There is one last set of basic estates that you should be familiar with that does not fit neatly into the above scheme: the estates created when a life estate is cut short.[119]

The material has already analyzed "cutting short" an estate when it looked at the fee simple determinable, fee simple subject to a condition subsequent, and fee simple subject to an executory limitation. In all three of those scenarios, the estate being cut short is a fee simple. Notice that analysis had to deal with only one issue: was the fee simple going to continue forever, or was it going to be cut short. In contrast, because a life estate by definition **must** end, if a life estate may also be cut short, there are two contingencies that must be dealt with: (1) who is going to get the life estate **if it ends naturally**; and (2) who is going to get the life estate **if it is cut short - if it ends prematurely**?

This point can be better understood by diagramming the concept of cutting short a life estate. First, an example of a life estate being cut short:

EXAMPLE 1

O → To A for life, but if A marries B, then to C and her heirs.

---

[119] Theoretically, fee tails and term of years can also be cut short. But the fee tail has been abolished for all practical purposes, and the term of years is best left for landlord-tenant law. If a finite estate is to be cut short, the norm is for the estate to be a life estate. The life estate discussion, however, in theory applies equally to the fee tail and the term of years. Just as we had fee simple defeasibles, we have finite estate defeasibles.

In the "life estate being cut short" scenario there are two points in time when we have to a ccount for the possibility that the right to possession may transfer hands from one party to another. First, if the condition cutting short the life estate occurs (indicated by the dashed cross line); and second, if the condition cutting short the life estate does not occur but the life estate ends naturally (indicated by the hard cross line):

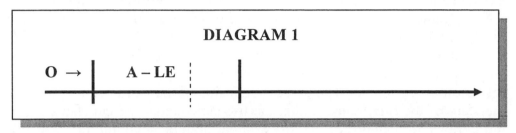

The analysis is not as bad as it looks. The key is to determine if the express words of limitation cutting short the life estate are **determinable** words of limitation or **condition subsequent** words of limitation.

II. THE LIFE ESTATE CUT SHORT BY DETERMINABLE WORDS OF LIMITATION.

If determinable words of limitation are used to cut short the life estate, the life estate determinable is treated like a life estate for analytical purposes. The classic determinable words of limitation again are **"as long as ... ."**[120] If determinable words of limitation are used to cut short the life estate, the **same party will hold the future interest whether the condition occurs or not.** The only question then is whether that future interest is held by the original grantor, O, or a third party.

If the future interest is held by the original grantor, "O," (either expressly or by default), then A holds a **life estate determinable** and O holds a **reversion in fee simple**:

---

[120] Notice these words of limitation come from the fee simple determinable words of limitation: "as long as/so long as/while/until/during ... ." Although the phrase "as long as" is the most commonly used of these possible words of limitation for cutting short a life estate, if any of them are used the above stated rule (that the same party will hold the future interest whether the condition occurs or not) still applies.

EXAMPLE 2

O → To A for life as long as she remains unmarried.

Because there is no express holder for the future interest, the original grantor (O) is deemed to have reserved the future interest. Because the words of limitation following the life estate are "as long as," O is deemed to hold the future interest whether the condition occurs or not (whether A marries or not). A's life estate is a life estate determinable, and O's future interest is a reversion in fee simple. The express inclusion of the word "determinable" in the state of the title indicates that the life estate could be cut short, and the term "reversion" indicates that the original grantor holds the future interest in either event (whether the life estate is cut short or if it ends naturally).

Similarly, if the express words of limitation "**as long as**" are used to cut short the life estate and there is an express reference to a **third party holding the future interest,** the common law deemed that the third party was to receive the future interest whether the condition occurred or not:

EXAMPLE 3

O → To A for life as long as she remains unmarried, then to
        B and her heirs.

Again, A was deemed to hold a **life estate determinable.** B was deemed to hold a **vested remainder in fee simple absolute.** The only change in the terminology describing the state of the title was the inclusion of the word "determinable" to reflect that the life estate may be cut short. Use of the term "remainder" following a life estate determinable indicated that the third party held the future interest whether the life estate was cut short or not. As long as the future interest is held by the same party (whether the condition cutting short the life estate occurs or not) the basic reversion/remainder terminology applies except the word "determinable" is added to the life estate to reflect that it may be cut short.

III. THE LIFE ESTATE CUT SHORT BY CONDITION SUBSEQUENT WORDS OF LIMITATION.

If the express words of limitation introducing the condition which may cut short the life estate are "but if ... ," the key again is who holds the future interest. But the analysis is a bit more complicated. The material will start with the straight forward and move to the more complicated.

First, if condition subsequent words of limitation are used to cut short the life estate, **and the future interest is held by the grantor**[121] whether the condition occurs or not, the future interest in the grantor is treated the same as if the life estate were not subject to being cut short. The life estate is called a **life estate subject to a condition subsequent** (to indicate that it may be cut short), and the grantor holds a **reversion** in fee simple.

EXAMPLE 4

O → To A for life, but if she marries, then the life estate ends.

O → To A for life, but if she marries, then to O and her heirs.

In both conveyances, A has a life estate subject to a condition subsequent, and O has a reversion in fee simple.

If, however, the **condition subsequent words of limitation** are used (typically "but if ... ") **and the express future interest is held by a third party**, a completely different analysis is performed.

EXAMPLE 5

O → To A for life, but if she marries, then to B and her heirs.

---

[121] Either expressly or by default

The key to understanding how to analyze such conveyances is to remember that where condition subsequent words of limitation (typically "but if, ...") are used to cut short the life estate, the courts generally construe such language as indicating that the third party is entitled to possession of the property **only if** the express condition occurs. If the condition does not occur, the grantor receives the right to possess the property after the life estate.   So the state of the title needs to account for both possible contingencies.   The life estate is a **life estate subject to an executory limitation** to indicate that it may be cut short in favor of a third party, the third party holds a **shifting executory interest** (typically in fee simple). Because the grantor will take possession of the property **only** if the condition subsequent does **not** occur, the grantor will take possession **only** if the life estate ends naturally. Thus, the grantor holds a **reversion** in fee simple.[122]

Returning to our example, under this scenario, there are two, mutually exclusive, potential takers of the future interest. The state of the title is that A has a **life estate subject to an executory limitation,** B has a **shifting executory interest** in fee simple, and O has a **reversion** in fee simple absolute.

IV. RECAP

The keys to analyzing the life estate which may be cut short are: (1) determining whether **determinable** or **condition subsequent** words of limitation are used to cut short the life estate, and (2) determining if the future interest is held by the same party whether or not the condition occurs.

If the express condition which might cut short the life estate is introduced by the determinable words of limitation (typically "as long as"), the same party is deemed to hold the future interest whether the condition occurs or not. If this is the case and the future interest is expressly given to a third party, the life estate is a life estate determinable and the third party holds a remainder in fee simple. If there is no express taker for the future interest, or if it is expressly reserved by O, the original grantor, the life estate is a life estate determinable and the future interest is a reversion in the grantor.

---

[122] If the condition occurs, the life estate ends prematurely (immediately upon the condition occurring) and the right to possess the property passes to the express third party taker. If the condition does not occur, however, upon the natural end of the life estate the future interest falls to our default taker, the original grantor, O.

If the express condition is introduced by the condition subsequent words of limitation (typically "but if, ...") and the future interest is held, either expressly or implicitly, by the grantor, the life estate is a life estate subject to a condition subsequent and the future interest is a reversion in the grantor. If, however, the condition subsequent words of limitation are used and the future interest is expressly given to a third party, then the common law deemed that the third party received the right to possession only if the condition occurred; and if it did not, the grantor received the right to possession upon the natural end of the life estate. The life tenant held a life estate subject to an executory limitation, the third party held a shifting executory interest in fee simple, and the grantor held a reversion in fee simple.

PROBLEM SET 9

State the title to the following problems:

1.   O →   To A for life as long as A does not attend business school.

2.   O →   To A for life as long as A does not attend business school, then to B and her heirs.

3.   O →   To A for life, but if A attends business school, then to B and her heirs.

Chapter 10

MISCELLANEOUS COMMON LAW RULES REGULATING CONVEYANCES

I. OVERVIEW

Although we take for granted the right to inherit property, at early common law there was no such right. The king owned all the land, and grants were only in life estate. In time, however, grantees negotiated for the right of inheritance (the right[123] for the property to pass to their heirs); but if the property did pass by inheritance, the heirs had to pay what amounted to an inheritance tax.[124] The inheritance tax applied, however, **only** if a party **inherited** the property. With time, grantees and their lawyers attempted to manipulate the scheme of possessory estates and future interests in an attempt to avoid this inheritance tax. There were two conveyances which grantees used in an attempt to avoid the dreaded inheritance tax. The common law courts, however, developed a special rule which applies to each such scenario to prohibit such avoidance.

II. RULES FURTHERING COMMON LAW INHERITANCE TAX

A. THE RULE IN SHELLEY'S CASE

Assume O own a piece of property that she want to give to A, with the expectation that upon A's death the property will go to A's heirs. O could simply convey it to A in fee simple absolute:

EXAMPLE 1

O → To A and her heirs.

---

[123] But not the obligation – hence the heirs take *no* property interest while the grantee *is* alive, only the expectation of the right to take the property upon the grantee's death if he or she does not transfer it *inter vivos or* devise it to another.

[124] Technically it is called a "relief."

But then upon A's death, the property would be inherited by A's heirs who would have to pay the dreaded inheritance tax. What if, however, O conveyed only a life estate to A, and a remainder to the heirs of A?

EXAMPLE 2

O → To A for life, then to the heirs of A and their heirs.

The heirs of A would **not** take through inheritance but rather through the express conveyance. Thus the grantor arguably could avoid the feudal inheritance tax.

The common law courts saw through this conveyance, however, and adopted what came to be known as the Rule in Shelley's Case to close this loophole. Under the **Rule in Shelley's Case, if a life estate is given to a party, and in the same instrument a REMAINDER is given to the life tenant's HEIRS, give the remainder to the life tenant (and check for merger)**.[125] The best way to apply the Rule in Shelley's Case is always to state the title of each conveyance as written. Returning to the example above, the state of the title as drafted is:

EXAMPLE 2A

O → To A for life, then to the heirs of A and their heirs.

A has a life estate;
A's heirs have a contingent remainder[126] in fee simple; and
O has a reversion in fee simple.

---

[125] Shelley's Case, 1 Co. Rep. 93b (1581); PROPERTY RESTATEMENT, *supra* note 10, at §§ 312-13. The parenthetical to check for merger is *not* a part of the Rule in Shelley's Case, but it is such a frequent by-product of the Rule that you should be sure to couple these two rules together for analytical purposes.

[126] The remainder is contingent because to qualify as an heir, the party must survive the decedent. As long as a person is alive, he or she has only heirs apparent, no heirs, because it cannot be determined who survived the party until he or she dies.

The life tenant is A, and the conveyance attempts to give a remainder to the heirs of A, the life tenant. The conveyance is a classic example of a conveyance falling within the scope of the Rule in Shelley's Case. Applying the Rule, give A the remainder. Because A is born, ascertainable, and there are no express condition precedents, A holds a vested remainder. Because the vested remainder is in fee simple, O's reversion is destroyed. Pursuant to the Rule in Shelley's Case, A now holds the life estate and a vested remainder in fee simple. Because A now holds two successive vested interests, the merger doctrine applies, and the life estate merges into the vested remainder in fee simple to give A a fee simple absolute. (Remember, merger is **not** part of the Rule in Shelley's case, but it often applies after the Rule in Shelley's case applies.)

The scope of the Rule in Shelley's Case is fairly narrow, however. First, the Rule applies only if the remainder is given to the heirs of the life tenant **in the same instrument** as the instrument creating the life estate. For example, in the above scenario, if the grantor gave A a life estate, and then – in another instrument/conveyance – conveyed the reversion to the apparent heirs of A, they would **not** be taking in the same instrument. The Rule in Shelley's Case would not apply.[127]

A second, and arguably more important, limitation on the scope of the Rule in Shelley's Case is that it applies only if a **remainder** is given to a life tenant's heirs. The Rule does not apply if an executory interest is given to a life tenant's heirs:

EXAMPLE 3

O → To A for life, then one day after A's death, to A's heirs and their heirs.

This conveyance presents the classic "gap" scenario. A has a life estate. O holds a reversion in fee simple subject to an executory limitation. And A's heirs hold a springing executory interest in fee simple. Because there is no remainder, the Rule in Shelley's Case does not apply.

---

[127] Under this scenario, the apparent heirs of A would not be taking by inheritance, but rather by separate conveyance from the grantor.

The third limitation on the Rule in Shelley's Case is that the life tenant's **heirs** must hold the remainder. If other relatives or individuals hold the remainder, the Rule does not apply. Accordingly, if the conveyance provides:

EXAMPLE 4

O → To A for life, then to A's children and their heirs.

The Rule in Shelley's Case would not apply. The remainder is held by A's children, not A's heirs. The Rule's application is limited to remainders held by a life tenant's **heirs.**

Lastly, if the Rule in Shelley's Case does apply, the merger doctrine **often** applies, but not always. For example:

EXAMPLE 5

O → To A for life, then to B for life, then to A's heirs and their heirs.

State the title:

EXAMPLE 5 TITLE

A: has a life estate,
B: has a vested remainder in life estate,
A's heirs: have a contingent remainder in fee simple, and
O: has a reversion in fee simple.

Because the heirs of one of the life tenants, A, are taking a remainder, give the remainder to the life tenant. Re-state the title:

EXAMPLE 5 RULE IN SHELLEY'S CASE TITLE

A: has a life estate,

B: has a vested remainder in life estate,

A: has a vested remainder in fee simple, and

O: has a reversion in fee simple.

Now check to see if the merger doctrine applies. A holds a life estate and a vested remainder in fee simple, but B's intervening vested remainder in life estate prevents merger. Merger is not an official part of the Rule in Shelley's Case, and although it often applies following the effect of the Rule in Shelley's Case, it does not always.

In conclusion, according to the Rule in Shelley's Case, if there is a **remainder** in the heirs of a **life tenant,** give the remainder to the life tenant (and check to see if merger applies).

B. THE DOCTRINE OF WORTHIER TITLE

The second conveyance where common law grantors tried to use to avoid the common law feudal "inheritance tax" was where a grantor purported to convey a future interest to the grantor's heirs:[128]

EXAMPLE 6

O $\rightarrow$ To A for life, then to the heirs of O and their heirs.[129]

---

[128] Assume O owns property, wants to convey a life estate to A, but wants to retain the future interest (a reversion). Assuming A is younger than O, and thus has a longer life expectancy, the more likely scenario is that the reversion will pass to O's heirs by inheritance before it becomes possessory again. O's heirs would have to pay the common law inheritance tax on it. If that is the likely scenario, O could try to avoid the inheritance tax by expressly conveying the future interest directly to O's heirs inter vivos. The Doctrine of Worthier Title was developed to block this type of tax avoidance.

[129] The state of the title as drafted would be: A has a life estate, the heirs of A have a contingent remainder in fee simple, and O would have a reversion in fee simple. Notice the remainder would have to be contingent, because the life tenant has no heirs while he or she is alive, only heirs apparent.

State the title:

EXAMPLE 6 TITLE

A: has a life estate,
O's heirs: have a contingent remainder in fee simple, and
O: has a reversion in fee simple.

Thus O's heirs would **not** take the property through inheritance but rather through the words of purchase in the conveyance. They could avoid the feudal "inheritance tax" if this type of conveyance were permitted.

The common law courts, however, were fairly protective of the feudal inheritance tax. They closed this loophole by developing the Doctrine of Worthier Title.[130] The **Doctrine of Worthier Title** is conceptually very similar to the Rule in Shelley's Case, only the Doctrine of Worthier Title applies to **any future interest (remainder or executory interest)** given to the **grantor's heirs. Under the Doctrine of Worthier Title, if an instrument conveys a possessory interest to a third party and the same instrument purports to give a remainder or executory interest to the grantor's HEIRS, give the future interest to the grantor (and check for merger).**[131] In the example above, if we give the contingent remainder to O, then it no longer is a contingent remainder but rather becomes a reversion in O in fee simple. If O were to die before A, and O did not dispose of the reversion by transfer or devise, the heirs of O would end up holding the future interest. O's heirs, however, would take the interest through their right of inheritance, subjecting them to the feudal inheritance tax.

Although there is some ambiguity as to the full scope of the Doctrine of Worthier Title, the better view appears to be that the doctrine applied not

---

[130] Technically, the Doctrine of Worthier Title is a rule of construction, not a rule of law. The significance of that difference, however, is beyond the scope of this coverage.

[131] The parenthetical to check for merger is **not** a part of the Doctrine of Worthier Title, but it is such a frequent by-product of the Doctrine that you should be sure to couple these two rules together.

only to remainders but also to executory interests. Assume the conveyance were as follows:

EXAMPLE 7

O → To A for life, then one day after A's death, to O's heirs and their heirs.

This conveyance presents the classic "gap" scenario. A has a life estate. O holds a reversion in fee simple subject to an executory limitation. And O's heirs hold a springing executory interest in fee simple. Because the Doctrine of Worthier Title applies not only to remainders but also to executory interests, apply the Doctrine. O would then hold the reversion in fee simple subject to an executory limitation and the springing executory interest in fee simple absolute. The springing executor interest and the reversion would merge. Thus, the title would be A holds a life estate, and O holds a reversion in fee simple absolute. If O dies without transferring or devising the interest, the practical effect will be the same as if the Doctrine were not applied. But O's heirs would be subject to the inheritance tax because they take by inheritance under the Doctrine, not as purchasers[132] under the words of purchase in the conveyance.

Just like the Rule in Shelley's Case, however, the Doctrine of Worthier Title applies only if the party holding the future interest is the original grantor's **heirs.** The Doctrine does not apply if the conveyance expressly gives the future interest to the grantor's "children," "nieces and nephews," or any other relatives or friends. Like the Rule in Shelley's Case, the Doctrine applies only where the avoidance is attempted in a single conveyance. If O conveys a life estate to A, and thereafter O transfers the reversion in a different *inter vivos* conveyance to O's heirs apparent, the Doctrine would not apply.

In conclusion, according to the Doctrine of Worthier Title, where a conveyance purports to convey **a future interest (remainder or executory interest)** to the **heirs of the grantor**, give the future interest to the grantor (and check to see if merger applies).

---

[132] By "purchasers" here the material does not mean in exchange for valuable consideration, but simply that they take pursuant to the express words of purchase in the conveyance as opposed to by inheritance.

III. RULE IN PUREFOY'S CASE

An inherent characteristic of executory interests is that they are indestructible, unlike contingent remainders which are destructible. A by-product of this difference was that at common law, a grantee of an ambiguous conveyance would prefer to have the conveyance construed as an executory interest rather than a contingent remainder.

For example:

EXAMPLE 8

O → To A for life, then to B and her heirs if B graduates from law school.

State the title. A has a life estate. But what about B? Does B have a contingent remainder in fee simple, in which case O would have a reversion in fee simple; or does B have a springing executory interest in fee simple, in which case O would have a reversion in fee simple subject to an executory limitation. In the event A's life estate ends before B graduates from law school, this distinction would make all the difference in the world to B because the common law courts ruled that contingent remainders were destructible but executory interests were not.[133] The **Rule in Purefoy's Case** established that if an interest could be characterized as either a contingent remainder or an executory interest (because the condition was such that it could occur during the prior life estate or it could occur after), the interest is deemed a contingent remainder subject to the destructibility of contingent remainders. The rationale behind the Rule in Purefoy's Case is that favoring the contingent remainder construction would mean that there was a chance that the interest would be destroyed, thereby cleaning up the state of the title and promoting the productive use of the land and its marketability.

---

[133] If the interest were construed as a contingent remainder and A's life estate ended before B graduated from law school, B's contingent remainder would be destroyed and B would be out of luck. On the other hand, if the interest were construed as an executory interest, it would not matter whether A's life estate was still possessory or not. All B had to do was graduate from law school for the interest to become possessory.

Today, many jurisdictions have abolished the common law destructibility of contingent remainder. In those jurisdictions, the contingent remainder is functionally indistinguishable from an executory interest for our purposes and the issue underlying the Rule in Purefoy's Case is moot.

In conclusion, according to the Rule in Purefoy's Case, where an **interest can be construed as either a contingent remainder or an executory interest, construe it as a contingent remainder**.

RECAP CHART

CATEGORY	POSSESSORY ESTATE	FUTURE INTEREST	
		GRANTOR	THIRD PARTY
FEE SIMPLE	FEE SIMPLE ABSOLUTE	NONE	NONE
FEE SIMPLE DEFEASIBLES	FEE SIMPLE DETERMINABLE	POSS REV	--
	FEE SIMPLE SUBJECT TO CONDITION SUBSEQUENT	RT of ENTRY/ POWER TERM	--
	FEE SIMPLE SUBJ TO EXEC LIM	--	EXEC INT
FINITE ESTATES	LIFE ESTATE	REVERSION	REMAINDER
	FEE TAIL	REVERSION	REMAINDER
	TERM OF YEARS	REVERSION	REMAINDER

1. Contingent rem: Must vest prior to, or at, the exp (incl merger/forfeiture/renun) of prec poss estate or it is destroyed
2. Alt cont rem: 1st cont rem must vest prior to merger/forfeiture/renun or both are destroyed
3. Vested rem: remainder must be 1) born, 2) ascertainable, and 3) no express condition precedent (same/prec clause)
4. Vested rem subj to divestmt: vested rem w/ express condition prec in clause subsequent to clause creating remainder
5. executory interests: shifting (3rd party to 3rd party) vs. springing (grantor to 3rd party: "gap"/future interest only)
6. Rule in Shelley's Case: If rem in heirs of life tenant, give rem to life tenant (check for merger)
7. Doc Worthier Title: If future int (rem or exec int) in heirs of grantor, give future int to grantor (check for merger)
8. Rule in Purefoy's Case: If conveyance can be construed as cont rem or exec int, construe as cont rem

PROBLEM SET 10

State the title to the following problems:

1. O → To A for life, then to A's heirs and their heirs.

2. O → To A for life, then to O's heirs and their heirs.

3. O → To A for life, then to O's heirs and their heirs one day after A's funeral.

4. O → To A for life, then to B for life, then to the heirs of A's body and their heirs.

5. O → To A for life, then to A's heirs and their heirs one day after A's funeral.

Chapter 11

CLASS GIFTS

I. OVERVIEW

For the most part, up to this point each grantee in the conveyances and examples has been an individual. But there is no requirement that this must be the case. A conveyance can be to more than one person or even to a class of individuals.[134]

EXAMPLE 1

O → To A and B and their heirs.

State the title: A and B hold the property **concurrently** in fee simple absolute. While there is a whole body of separate law entitled **concurrent estates** dealing with the different ways that multiple parties or classes of people may simultaneously hold the right to possess the same piece of property, the law of concurrent estates is beyond the scope of this material. The material is concerned only with **class gifts** to the extent they overlap with the possessory estate and future interest scheme developed so far. This overlap occurs primarily **where there is a conveyance of a remainder to a class; the issue is whether the remainder is vested or contingent**.

II. ANALYSIS

Returning to the three part test for vested remainders, is the grantee:
     (1) born,
     (2) ascertainable, and
     (3) is there any express condition precedent?[135]

---

[134] In large part, a "class" is distinguished from a mere collection of individuals by the common characteristic(s) of the members of the class.

[135] If the remainder fails any part of the test, it is contingent.

As applied to a single individual, the test is rather straight forward. But when applied to a class, the test is a bit more complicated. This fact becomes apparent when the test is applied to the following conveyance:

EXAMPLE 2

O → To A for life, then to B's children and their heirs.

State the title: A has a life estate, and B's children have a remainder in fee simple absolute. Is the remainder vested or contingent?

Like other conveyances where the recipient is *described generically* as opposed to named, the key is what additional information is given. Assume B has no children yet - would the remainder be vested or contingent? Contingent, because the children are not born or ascertainable. Because the remainder is contingent, O would also hold a reversion in fee simple.

Now assume, however, that B gives birth to a child, X. Apply the test. Well, as to X, she is born and ascertainable and there is no express condition precedent - so the remainder is vested. But because B is still alive, B could have more children. **Where there is a remainder to a class, once at least one class member vests, the remainder becomes vested. But if the class is such that more individuals can enter the class and vest in the property, the remainder is classified as *a vested remainder subject to open.*** The "*subject to open*" phrase indicates that more individuals may enter the class and vest in the property interest. As each new member of the class vests, the shares of each vested member is re-calculated so that each vested member holds an equal share.[136] The "vested remainder subject to open" remains open until the class *closes.*

---

[136] Thus, another way to describe the remainder is to say that it is vested *subject to partial divestment.* As each new member of the class vests, the share of the members who were already vested is reduced, or partially divested. MOYNIHAN, *supra* note 9, at 125-26.

III. CLOSING THE CLASS

A. NATURALLY/BIOLOGICALLY

There are basically two ways for a class to close. First, **a class closes when it becomes impossible for new members to enter the class.** The most common example of this is biological closure. Returning to the example above ("To A for life, then to B's children and their heirs"), once B dies, it is impossible for B to have any more children (the common law presumed that individuals were fertile up until death, so that biological closure did not occur until death of the class creating individual).[137] Assuming that A is still alive, once B dies, however many children B had is the size of the class and the class will close. There is no special terminology to indicate that the class is closed except we drop the phrase "subject to open." The remainder simply is vested.

B. RULE OF CONVENIENCE

The second method for a class to close is by the **rule of convenience**. The rule of convenience is exactly that, a convenient rule the common law courts created to avoid a whole host of potentially difficult legal and administrative questions. Some background will help understand the rule. Returning to the example above ("To A for life, then to B's children and their heirs"), assume A is still alive, B is still alive, and B has two children: X and Y. State the title:

> A has a life estate, and
> B's children, X and Y, have a vested remainder, subject to open, in fee simple.[138]

Now assume A dies, but B is still alive. Because B is still alive, more individuals can enter the class. But what about the property?

---

[137] Posthumously born children, however, can also qualify as a child of the deceased husband if the child is born within 280 days of the husband's death. The common law (and still general rule) is that for inheritance purposes, a child who qualifies as a posthumously born child is considered as alive from the moment of conception.

[138] Notice there is no need for a reversion in O because the remainder in fee simple is vested in at least one individual. Even if B has no more children and X and Y die before A, because X and Y's interests are vested their shares would pass to their heirs or devises.

Notice the quandary the courts were in. When A dies, somebody has to have the right to enter and possess the property. X and Y hold the vested remainder, but what can they do with the property if there is a chance that they may have to share it if B has more children in the future? Can they transfer their interest if they do not know what their share will be until B dies? If they put the property to profitable use, must they share the profits with future children of B? Rather than dealing with these and other potentially difficult legal and administrative questions, the common law courts created the **rule of convenience**, which provides that **once one member of the class is entitled to take actual possession of the property, the class closes**. Even though B is biologically capable of having more children, the moment X and Y become entitled to actual possession of the property, the class closes. If one year later,[139] B has a child Z, Z has no right to claim an interest in the property. X and Y would hold the property jointly in fee simple absolute.

One last wrinkle on the class conveyances. A class conveyance can be coupled with an express condition precedent:

EXAMPLE 3

O → To A for life, then to B's children who survive A and
        their heirs.

Assume A is alive, B is alive, and B has two children,
C and D.

State the title. A has a life estate. "B's children" means that the remainder is held by a class, and because there is at least one member of the class you might be tempted to state that B's children hold a vested remainder subject to open. But notice there is an express condition precedent that only those children of B who survive A are entitled to the property. The express condition precedent means the remainder is contingent. If there is a remainder held by a class and there are members of the class born and ascertainable, that does not necessarily mean that the class interest is vested subject to open.

---

[139] At common law, a child was treated as alive from the moment of conception if it were to the child's advantage. Thus, a child in utero was treated as alive for purposes of construing conveyances.

You still must check to see if there is an express condition precedent which applies to the class. If there is, the remainder will remain contingent until the express condition is satisfied.

C. RECAP

Class conveyances present some challenges when determining whether a remainder is vested or contingent. The basic three part test for vested remainders applies, but the wrinkle is that more people may enter the class. Assuming there is no express condition precedent, if no member of the class is born and ascertainable, the class will remain contingent until the first member is born and ascertainable. Once one member of the class is born and ascertainable, the class becomes vested subject to open to reflect the fact that more members may join the class before it closes. The class closes either naturally (the source for new members no longer exists) or under the rule of convenience: the moment one class member is entitled to claim possession of his or her share.

CATEGORY	POSSESSORY ESTATE	FUTURE INTEREST	
		GRANTOR	THIRD PARTY
FEE SIMPLE	FEE SIMPLE ABSOLUTE	NONE	NONE
FEE SIMPLE DEFEASIBLES	FEE SIMPLE DETERMINABLE	POSS REV	--
	FEE SIMPLE SUBJECT TO CONDITION SUBSEQUENT	RT of ENTRY/ POWER TERM	--
	FEE SIMPLE SUBJECT TO AN EXECUTORY LIMITATION	--	EXEC INT
FINITE ESTATES	LIFE ESTATE	REVERSION	REMAINDER
	FEE TAIL	REVERSION	REMAINDER
	TERM OF YEARS	REVERSION	REMAINDER

1. Contingent rem: Must vest prior to, or at, the exp (incl merger/forfeiture/renun) of prec poss estate or it is destroyed
2. Alt cont rem: 1st cont rem must vest prior to merger/forfeiture/renun or both are destroyed
3. Vested rem: remainder must be 1) born, 2) ascertainable, and 3) no express condition precedent (same/prec clause)
4. Vested rem subj to divestmt: vested rem w/ express condition prec in clause subsequent to clause creating remainder
5. executory interests: shifting (3rd party to 3rd party) vs. springing (grantor to 3rd party: "gap"/future interest only)
6. Rule in Shelley's Case: If rem in heirs of life tenant, give rem to life tenant (check for merger)
7. Doc Worthier Title: If future int (rem or exec int) in heirs of grantor, give future int to grantor (check for merger)
8. Rule in Purefoy's Case: If conveyance can be construed as cont rem or exec int, construe as cont rem
9. Class gifts – vested subject to open: closure either naturally or rule of convenience

PROBLEM SET 11

State the title for each of the following problems. (Assume that the factual information set forth in sub parts a) through e) are **cumulative**):

1.   O →   To A for life, then to A's children and their heirs.

a)   Assume A is alive and has no children.

b)   Assume A has a child B.

c)   Assume B dies, survived by a child X.

d)   Assume A has a second child C.

e)   Assume A dies.

2.   O → To A for life, then to B's children and their heirs.

   a)   Assume A is alive and B has no children.

   b)   Assume B has a child X.

   c)   Assume B has a child Y.

   d)   Assume A dies, then B has a child Z.

REVIEW PROBLEM SET 12

State the title to the following problems:

1.   O →   To A and her heirs.

2.   O →   To A forever, then to B forever, then to C and her heirs.

3.   O →   To A and the female heirs of her body, then to B in fee simple absolute, then to O and her heirs.

4.   O →   To A and her heirs as long as the land is used for agricultural purposes, then to B and her heirs.

5.   O →   To A and her heirs, but if A sells alcohol on the property, then X and her heirs shall have the right to enter and claim the land.

6.   O →   To A for life, then to B and her heirs if B graduates from medical school.

   a.   Assume A and B are alive.

   b.   Assume A dies and B has not graduated from medical school.

7.   O →   To A for life, then to B and her heirs if B graduates from medical school, otherwise to C and her heirs.

       a.   Assume A and B are alive.

       b-1.   Assume A dies and B has not graduated from medical school.

       b-2.   Assume A renounces her interest and B has not graduated from medical school yet.

       b-3.   Assume B graduates from medical school, then B dies, and then A dies.

8.   O →   to A for life, then to B and her heirs if B attends A's funeral.

9.   O →   To A for life, but if B graduates from medical school, then to B and her heirs.

10.   O →   To A for life, then to B and her heirs as long as B farms the land.

11.   O →   To A for life, then to B and her heirs, but if B stops farming the land, then O may reenter and reclaim the land.

12.   O →   To A for life, then to B and her heirs, but if A stops farming the land, then to C and her heirs.

13.   O →   To A for life, then to A's grandchildren and their heirs.

     a.   Assume A has no grandchildren.

     b.   Assume A has a grandchild X.

     c.   Assume A has another grandchild Y.

     d.   Assume X dies and then Y dies.

15.   O →   To A for life, then to B and her heirs, but if B stops farming the land, then O can re-enter and reclaim the land.

16.   O →   To A for life, then to B and her heirs as long as the land is farmed, then to C and her heirs.

17.   O →   To A for life, then to B and her heirs, but if B stops farming the land, then to C and her heirs.

18.   O →   To A for life, then to B and her heirs, but if A stops farming the land, then to C and her heirs.

19.   O →   To A for life, then to B and her heirs, but if B marries C, then to X and her heirs.

     (a)   Assume A, B, C and X are alive.

     (b)   Assume A dies and B, C and X are alive.

20.   O →   To A for life, then to B and her heirs if B graduates from law school.

     (a)   Assume A and B are both alive and B has not graduated from law school yet.

21.   O →   To A for life, then to B and her heirs if B attends A's funeral.

22.   O →   To A for life, then to B and her heirs if B graduates from law school.

   (a)   Assume A has died and B has not graduated from law school yet.

23.   O →   To A for life, then to A's heirs and the heirs of their body.

24.   O →   To A for life, then to B for life, then to A's heirs and the heirs of their body.

25.   O →   To A for life, then to A's heirs and the heirs of their body if A survives B.

26.   O →   To A for life, then to A's heirs and their heirs who attend A's funeral.

27.   O →   To A for life, then to O's heirs and the heirs of their body.

28.   O →   To A for life, then to B for life, then to O's heirs and the heirs of their body.

29.   O →   To A for life, then to O's heirs and the heirs of their body if A survives B.

30.   O →   To A for life, then to A's heirs and their heirs if they spread A's ashes across the Pacific Ocean.

31.   O →   To A for life as long as A does not attend medical school.

32.   O →   To A for life as long as A does not attend medical school, then
              to B and her heirs.

33.   O →   To A for life, but if A attends medical school, then to B and her
              heirs.

Chapter 12

THE RULE AGAINST PERPETUITIES

I. OVERVIEW

As you probably have noticed, the scheme of possessory estates and future interests gives a property owner the ability to control, to some extent, the property even after conveying the possessory interest to another. This control is manifested in the conditions the grantor puts on the possessory estate and/or future interests in the express terms of the conveyance. For example:

EXAMPLE 1

O → To A and her heirs as long as she farms the land, then
to B and her heirs.

A has a fee simple subject to an executory limitation, and B has a shifting executory interest in fee simple.

O continues to exert some control over the property after the conveyance because of the condition O put into the conveyance. A and her heirs have an incentive to continue to use the land as a farm because if they stop farming the land their right to the land will be forfeited, and B and her heirs will have the right to claim possession of the property. The problem is that the grantor's wish as to how the land should be used may not be the highest or best use of the land. Even assuming, *arguendo*, that agricultural use was the highest and best use of the land when the conveyance was created, over time conditions change. Agricultural use may no longer be the highest or best use. If one thinks of the suburban sprawl that occurred following World War II, when farmland was converted to residential use, just think what would have happened if some (or even all) of the land in question had been restricted to agricultural use only. Even without the benefit of formalized law and economics training, the common law courts realized that there had to be a limit on such control by a grantor or the property might not be put to its best use, and society in general would suffer.

To a large degree a grantor's ability to control the property through express conditions in the conveyance is limited by the transferability of the different possessory estates and future interests. If one party comes along and purchases the possessory estate and the future interest, through the merger doctrine the property would be freed from any such conditions. The new owner would be free to use the property as he or she wished. But because contingent remainders, executory interests and vested remainders subject to open were not transferable, the common law courts had to come up with a different rule to limit their effect. The common law courts were not adverse to some control by a grantor, but the courts reasoned that after a **certain amount of time,** current owners of the possessory estate should be capable of freeing themselves from these conditions, thereby being free to use the property as they wished and/or in the best interests of society. Accordingly, the courts concluded that the at the latest, contingent remainders, executory interests, and vested remainders subject to open **had to** "vest," if at all, within the "lives in being"[140] plus twenty one years or the future interest was void from its attempted creation.

Although the rationale underlying the Rule against Perpetuities is rather comprehensible (to limit the ability of the grantor to exercise control over the property after conveying it), the mechanics of the rule are somewhat more difficult.

II.   THE CREATE, KILL, & COUNT APPROACH

The Rule against Perpetuities provides that: "No interest is good unless it must vest, if at all, not later than twenty-one years after some life in being at the creation of the interest." Although this express statement of the Rule is so technical it is difficult to comprehend, once the rule is broken down, the Rule is more comprehensible.

First, although the Rule states that "[n]o **interest** is good ... ," the Rule against Perpetuities does not apply to the vast majority of

---

[140] The "lives in being" constitute *anybody* who was alive at the time of the conveyance – the duration of that person's life. The material will elaborate on the components of the Rule against Perpetuities shortly.

possessory estates and future interests. The Rule against Perpetuities applies **only** to:

(1) contingent remainders,
(2) executory interests, and
(3) vested remainders subject to open.[141]

Second, the Rule requires these interests "vest, if at all ... ." Although as a technical matter to say that these interests must vest means different things for each interest,[142] as a general rule the interest vests if it has the right to become **POSSESSORY.** (This general rule does not apply in all cases because in a small number of cases a contingent remainder may vest without becoming possessory. We will discuss these exceptions to the general rule in greater detail later.)[143]

And third, the future interest must become possessory, if at all, "not later than twenty-one years after some life in being at the creation of the interest." It is this third component of the Rule which creates most of the problems in understanding the Rule. This phrase constitutes the time limit the common law courts settled upon for how long the future interests may tie up the property – for "some life in being at the creation of the interest" plus "twenty-one years." This time limit is analogous to a statute of limitations. The future interest subject to the Rule must vest, if at all, by that point in time (the lives in being at the time the interest was created plus twenty one years - the perpetuities period) or the interest is void.

There are, however, two important points to note about the Rule against Perpetuities time limit which distinguish it from the typical statute of limitations.[144] First, unlike the typical statute of limitations

---

[141] The Rule against Perpetuities applies to other interests, such as powers of appointments and options to purchase, but those interests are beyond the scope of our introductory materials.

[142] To say that these three different interests must "vest" means different things with respect to the different future interests:

1) contingent remainders must vest or fail,
2) executory interests must become possessory, and
3) vested remainders subject to open must close and completely vest

[143] You will see that the "must become POSSESSORY" shortcut works for everything but conveyances with two successive contingent remainders.

[144] And it is these two points which combine to create most of the problems in

where the time period is a set number of years, the time limit under the Rule against Perpetuities is a formula: the lives in being at the creation of the interest plus 21 years. But how long is that? How do the courts calculate that time limit? (Beginning to see the difficulty with the Rule against Perpetuities?)

The second point about the Rule against Perpetuities time limit which distinguishes it from the typical statute of limitations is how the time limit is applied. Under the typical statute of limitations, the courts wait to see if the claim has been brought within the statutory period in question. The statute of limitations comes into play to bar the claim only if the claim has not been brought by the end of the statutory period, but is asserted thereafter. For example, if the statute of limitations for bringing a wrongful termination cause of action is 5 years, the statute of limitations does not kick into effect unless 5 years has passed, and then the plaintiff files his or her cause of action for wrongful termination. The statute of limitations would come into effect and bar the cause of action.

In contrast, under the Rule against Perpetuities, the perpetuities period comes into play and is applied to the future interest **the moment the future interest is created.** Under the traditional common law approach, there was no waiting. Testing the interest immediately upon creation required the courts to identify the relevant measuring life or lives to see if the interest would vest, if at all, within 21 years of the death of the measuring life or lives. Much has been written on (1) how to pick the right individual(s) who were alive at the time of the creation of the interest who should be used as "measuring lives;" and (2) how to test to see if the interest would vest, if at all, within 21 years of their death. The material will offer an alternative analytical approach.

The essence of the Rule against Perpetuities is that the future interest in question **must** vest, if at all, *within the lives in being at the creation of the interest plus 21 years*, or the interest is void from the moment of its attempted creation. Rather than thinking of all the different possible ways that the interest may vest within this time period, approach it from the opposite perspective: **If you can conceive of 1 possible scenario, no matter how implausible, where the interest could vest but ONLY AFTER the lives in being plus 21 years, the interest violates the Rule against Perpetuities.** In attempting to create such a scenario, you should

understanding the Rule.

use the **CREATE, KILL and COUNT** strategy.

Under the **CREATE, KILL and COUNT** approach, the first step is to create someone in whom the interest can vest, but only after the perpetuities time period. By creating this person *after* the conveyance, he or she cannot qualify as a life in being for purposes of the perpetuities time period. Second, kill everyone who was alive at the time of the conveyance. By killing everybody who was alive at the time the property interest was created, we take care of all the possible lives in being so we do not have to worry about identifying the right measuring life.[145] Then, count twenty-one years. Killing everybody who was alive at the time the property interest was created takes care of the "lives in being" part of the rule, but the time period is "the lives in being **plus 21 years.**" If it is **conceivable (no matter how absurd the scenario sounds)** that one of the parties created can claim possession of the property under the future interest in question, **BUT ONLY AFTER** the lives in being plus 21 years have expired - then we have violated the Rule against Perpetuities and the interest is void from the moment of its attempted creation. **If we CANNOT create a scenario in which the property interest becomes possessory in a party we created BUT ONLY AFTER the lives in being plus 21 years, then the property interest does NOT VIOLATE the Rule against Perpetuities and the interest is valid.** Enough of the theoretical description of the approach, time to apply it.

A. CONTINGENT REMAINDERS

State the title to the following conveyance:

EXAMPLE 2

O → To A for life, then to B and her heirs.

---

[145] If it helps, take a picture of all the people identified by name in the conveyance or in the additional facts to the conveyance. Then **create** as many people as you need in order to create a scenario in which one of the people you created will vest in the property but only after the lives in being plus 21 years. Then **kill** all the people who were in your picture (all the lives in being when the interest was created). Then **count** 21 years and see if you can create a scenario in which one of the people you created can claim possession of the property under the interest in question.

A has a life estate, and B has a vested remainder in fee simple absolute. Does the Rule against Perpetuities apply? No. Remember that you only have to worry about the Rule against Perpetuities if you see one of the three future interests subject to Rule: contingent remainders, executory interests, and/or vested remainders subject to open.

State the title to the following conveyance:

EXAMPLE 3

O →   To A for life, then to A's first child to reach age 25
and his or her heirs.

Assume A has two children, B age 23 and C age 20.

A has a life estate. A's first child to reach age 25 has a contingent remainder in fee simple, and O has a reversion in fee simple. Is there a future interest which is subject to the Rule against Perpetuities? Yes, the contingent remainder. Does the contingent remainder violate the Rule?

Your gut instinct is probably that the contingent remainder cannot violate the Rule. The time period is lives in being plus 21 years, and B is only two years away from vesting. But not so fast. The Rule against Perpetuities is a harsh rule that is not concerned with probabilities. If there is **any** possible scenario in which the contingent remainder will vest, but not until **after** the running of the Rule's time period, the interest is void. B and C could be killed in a car accident tomorrow, so it is possible that it could be quite a while before the interest vests. Having now shown you that you cannot jump to assumptions, work through the mechanics of the **"create, kill, and count"** approach.

First, **create** a new life in being (or as the case may be, lives in being). Who should that person be? **You should create someone who will be eligible to claim the interest. If the interest is to vest in someone other than a child, create as far back in the chain of eligible persons as possible.** For example, if the interest was "to A's first grandchild to reach age 21," and A were still alive and had two grandchildren, do not create another grandchild for A, create another child for A. Remember, the goal with the **create, kill and count** approach is to create a scenario which *will* violate the rule. If we fail in our quest, then and only then is the interest in the conveyance valid.

Back to the example above:

EXAMPLE 3

O →   To A for life, then to A's first child to reach age 25 and his or her heirs.

Assume A has two children, B age 23 and C age 20.

State the title. A has a life estate. A's first child to reach age 25 has a contingent remainder in fee simple, and O has a reversion in fee simple.

The contingent remainder at issue is to A's first child to reach age 25. So whom do we **create**? We want to create someone who is eligible to claim the property under the terms of the conveyance so create a new child for A: child X is born to A. We now have a life in being who was not alive at the time of the creation of the interest. What do we do next? Kill! Kill whom? All of the people who were alive at the time of the creation of the interest: A, B, C and everybody else in the world.[146] Then what? That takes care of the lives in being, but we still have to take care of the rest of the time period - **count** 21 years. How old is child X at the end of the Rule's time period? 21 years old. Is it conceivable that X will live another four years and be entitled to claim the property? Yes. Have we created a scenario in which the interest vests/becomes possessory after the lives in being plus 21 years? Yes. Therefore, the future interest violates the Rule against Perpetuities and is void from its attempted creation. The state of the title is A has a life estate and O has a reversion in fee simple. **(Notice that in applying the create, kill, and count approach to the contingent remainder, you suspend the destructibility of contingent remainders rule.)**

---

[146] Again, an easy way to identify all the lives in being is to take a picture of all the people identified in the conveyance and the factual information concerning the time of the conveyance.

Applying the rule to a few more problems involving contingent remainders will help you get comfortable with the approach. State the title for the following conveyance:

EXAMPLE 4

O →   To A for life, then to B and her heirs if B reaches age 25.

Assume B is age 23.

A has a life estate. B has a contingent remainder in fee simple, and O has a (default) reversion in fee simple. Because B's remainder is contingent, it is subject to the Rule against Perpetuities. Apply the **create, kill, and count** approach. Can you create someone who will be eligible to claim the property? No. The condition is tied to B; B is the only person who is eligible to satisfy the condition. **If you cannot create someone who would be eligible to satisfy the condition, then you cannot create a scenario which violates the Rule and the interest must be valid. If the condition is expressly tied to a** *named person* **who is** *alive*, **as opposed to a described person, the interest will not violate the Rule against Perpetuities.**[147]

State the title for the following conveyance:

EXAMPLE 5

O →   To A for life, then to A's heirs and their heirs if B reaches age 25.

Assume B is age 23.

---

[147] This is the first of several principles which results from the create, kill and count analysis. While the hope is that these principles help, if you understand the create, kill and count analysis and the mechanics of how to apply it, you do not need to memorize these principles. One of the beauties of the create, kill and count approach is its simplicity. This would be undermined by requiring you to memorize a set of related principles. All you need to know is whether the interest violates the Rule against Perpetuities, not the related principles.

The contingent remainder in A's oldest child who survives A is subject to the Rule against Perpetuities. Apply the **create, kill and count approach.** Can you create someone who will be eligible to claim the property? Yes, a new child X for A. Move to the next step - kill off all the lives in being who were alive at the time the interest was created: A, B, C and the rest of the world. Move to the next step - count 21 years and see if the interest will vest **but only after** the Rule's time period. Will it? **No.** X will be vested in the property and be eligible to claim possession, but that occurred the moment A died. There is no way to delay that until after the lives in being plus 21 years. Because we cannot create a scenario which vests/becomes possessory **but only after** the lives in being plus 21 years, the interest is valid. **If the remainder must vest, if at all, upon the death of the life tenant, it is impossible to create a scenario which vests/becomes possessory** after **the lives in being plus 21 years and thus the interest must be valid.**

One more point to note about the Rule against Perpetuities. Because the test is whether the interest vests within the lives in being at the time the interest is created, **it is critical that you determine when an instrument conveying a property interest becomes operative.** *Inter vivos* conveyances are typically by deed, and a deed is effective when it is properly delivered. Testamentary conveyances are by will, and a will is not effective until the testator dies. The following conveyances will highlight the importance of this distinction:

EXAMPLE 6

O → To A for life, then to O's first grandchild and his or her heirs.

Assume O has three children but no grandchildren.

State the title. A has a life estate. O's first grandchild has a contingent remainder in fee simple (contingent because he or she is not born and ascertainable), and O has a reversion in fee simple.

If this conveyance is by *inter vivos* deed, is the contingent remainder valid? Again, the first step is to create a new person, and our goal is to violate the Rule so create as far back in the process as possible.

Create a new child for O, X. Next, kill all the people who were alive at the time of the *inter vivos* conveyance: O, A, and O's 3 children. Then we count 21 years. Is it possible that X will have a child thereafter? Yes. Because that grandchild will be eligible to claim possession of the property under the contingent remainder, but **only after** the lives in being plus 21 years has passed, the contingent remainder is invalid.

What if the conveyance were by will? When O properly executes the will during O's life, the will still has no effect. No property interests are created at that point in time. The will is not effective until the party who executed the will dies. At that point, the will becomes effective. A now holds a life estate, with a contingent remainder in O's first grandchild. Is the contingent remainder valid? Put it to the test. First, create someone. Can we create a new child, X, for O? No. O is dead, so we can not create a new child. Create a grandchild, but then the interest would vest immediately, not after the lives in being plus 21 years. Because it is impossible to create a scenario where the interest vests but only after the lives in being plus 21 years, the contingent remainder is valid. (Concluding the interest is valid does not mean it will necessary vest. O's three children may die without having a child, but the interest will still be valid because it will vest, **if at all,** within the lives in being plus 21 years). Notice how the contingent remainder is valid if created by will, but invalid if created by deed inter vivos.

The last wrinkle concerning the Rule against Perpetuities and contingent remainders is the stacked contingent remainders conveyance. State the title for the following conveyance:

EXAMPLE 7

O →   To A for life, then to A's oldest child who survives
        her for life, then to A's oldest grandchild then living
        and his or her heirs.

        Assume A is alive and has two children: B age 45,
        and C age 50.

A has a life estate. A's oldest child who survives A has a contingent remainder in life estate, A's oldest grandchild who survives A's oldest child who survived A has a contingent remainder in fee simple, and O has a reversion in fee simple.

The first point to note is that there are two interests subject to the Rule against Perpetuities: the two contingent remainders. With respect to the first contingent remainder, although we can create a new child for A, the interest must vest, if at all, when we kill all the lives in being. There is no scenario in which we can delay the vesting of the interest until **after** the lives in being plus 21 year. Because we *cannot* create a scenario under the create, kill, and count approach which violates the Rule against Perpetuities, the interest is valid.

With respect to the second contingent remainder, however, we can create a new child for A, X. Then kill all the lives in being, count 21 years, and envision a scenario in which X has a child Y, who would be A's grandchild. When X dies thereafter, the second contingent remainder would vest in Y, but **only after** the running of the lives in being plus 21 years time period. Here, because we *can* create a scenario under the create, kill, and count approach where the interest vests, but only after the perpetuities time period, the interest is void. **When contingent remainders are stacked one after the other, the second remainder typically will be void unless it vests upon the first contingent remainder becoming possessory.** This principle is borne out in the next two examples.

State the title for the following examples:

EXAMPLE 8

O → To A for life, then to A's widow for life, then to A's children and their heirs.

O → To A for life, then to A's widow for life, then to A's children then living and their heirs.

Assume A is alive and has two children: B age 45, and C age 50.

In both conveyances, A has a life estate; A's widow has a contingent remainder in life estate; A's children have a contingent remainder in fee simple; and O has a reversion in fee simple. Again we have two contingent remainders which are subject to the Rule against Perpetuities. With respect to the first contingent remainder in A's widow, although we can create a new person X and have A marry that person so at the time of A's death that person is A's widow, her contingent remainder must vest, if at all, upon the expiration of the lives in being. There is no way to delay its vesting until after the 21 years, so the first contingent remainder is valid.

The second contingent remainder in A's children is trickier. First, note the subtle but critical difference in the wording of the second contingent remainder between the two conveyances. The first conveyance is simply to "A's children ...", the second is to "A's children *then* living ... ." The first contingent remainder will vest upon A's death (it will not become possessory until after the death of A's widow, but it will vest upon A's death). The second contingent remainder in the second conveyance, on the other hand, will not vest until after the death of A's widow because of the express condition that it is only the children of A **then living.** Put it to the test. Create a new person X. Have X and A marry and have a new child Y. Then kill off all the lives in being. Count 21 years. Y's interest is still a contingent remainder. Is it possible that **only after** the 21 years X, the widow, will die and Y's interest will become vested and possessory? Yes. Thereafter, the contingent remainder in "A's children then living" is void.[148] **(The first conveyance also shows why it is only a general rule that vested means becomes possessory. Where contingent remainders are stacked, the second contingent remainder can become vested even though it is not possessory. The interest only has to vest within the Rule against Perpetuities, it does not necessarily have to become possessory. So while it is easier to think of vested as meaning possessory, you can not do that where there are stacked contingent remainders.)**

---

[148] In Wills & Trusts circles this type of conveyance is commonly known as the "unborn widow" problem.

THE RULE AGAINST PERPETUITIES CONTINGENT
REMAINDER PROBLEM SET – PROBLEM SET 13

For each of the following problems, (1) state the title of the conveyance as drafted, (2) state if any of the interests are subject to the Rule against Perpetuities, and (3) state if the interest violates the Rule.

1.   O →   To A for life, then to B and her heirs if B reaches 25.

                   Assume B is 5.

2.   O →   To A for life, then to A's first child and his or her heirs.

                   Assume A has no children yet.

3.   O →   To A for life, then to A's first child to reach age 30 and his or her heirs.

                   Assume A has 2 children: B, age 25, and C, age 28.

4.   O →   To A for life, then to A's first child to reach age 21 and his or her heirs.

                   Assume A has 2 children: B, age 19, and C, age 18.

5.   O →   To A for life, then to A's first grandchild and his or her heirs.

Assume A has 6 children and no grandchildren.

6.   O devises Greenacres to A for life, then to O's first grandchild and his or her heirs.

Assume O has no grandchildren yet, but 5 children.

7.   O →   To A for life, then to B's first child to graduate from law school and his or her heirs.

Assume B has two children, and one of them is second year law student.

8.   O →   To A for life, then to A's widow for life, then to A's children who survive A's widow and their heirs.

9.   O →   To A for life, then to A's widow for life, then to A's children and their heirs.

B. EXECUTORY INTERESTS.

As complicated as the Rule against Perpetuities is as applied to contingent remainders, it is that easy as applied to executory interests. Remember, there are basically four different scenarios in which there may be an executory interest: (1) following a fee simple defeasible where the future interest is in a third party; (2) following a "future interest only" conveyance; (3) following a vested remainder subject to divestment; and (4) following the "gap" scenario.

1. The Rule against Perpetuities applied to the executory interest following a fee simple defeasible where the future interest is in a third party.

The most common executory interest is the shifting executory interest following a fee simple subject to an executory limitation:

EXAMPLE 9

O →   To A and her heirs as long as alcohol is not sold on the land, then to B and his heirs.

O →   To A and her heirs, but if alcohol is sold on the land, then to B and his heirs.

State the title.   In both conveyance, A has a fee simple subject to an executory limitation, and B has a shifting executory interest in fee simple.

Now that we know executory interests are subject to the Rule against Perpetuities, put B's shifting executory interest to the **create, kill and count** test. First, create - who? - X, an heir of A, and Y, an heir of B. Then **kill** A and B (and assume that the respective interests are inherited by their respective heirs, X and Y). Now **count** 21 years. Is it possible that X, who now holds the fee simple subject to an executory limitation, could sell alcohol on the land, thereby making Y's executory interest possessory? Yes. Therefore, B's executory interest in fee simple is void.

But that would seem to invalidate all executory interests in such fee simple defeasible scenarios. Yes, if the limiting condition is not tied to a life in being. Re-draft the conveyances just slightly:

EXAMPLE 10

O →   To A and her heirs as long as A does not sell alcohol on the land, then to B and his heirs.

O →   To A and her heirs, but if A sells alcohol on the land, then to B and his heirs.

State the title. Again, in both conveyances, A has a fee simple subject to an executory limitation, and B has a shifting executory interest in fee simple.

Notice, in these drafts of essentially the same conveyances, the restricting condition is expressly tied to a life in being, A. Thus the executory interest can only become possessory, if at all, during the lifetime of a life in being. It is impossible for the executory interest to become possessory only after the lives in being plus 21 years. The executory interest is valid.

Where the executory interest is following a fee simple defeasible (with the future interest in a third party), the executory interest will violate the Rule against Perpetuities unless the restricting condition is expressly tied to a life in being.

One variation on the fee simple defeasible with the future interest in a third party is where the grantor retains possession until a stated condition occurs. The classic variation on that scenario for Rule against Perpetuities purposes is as follows:

EXAMPLE 11

O's will states: To my descendants living at the time my estate is distributed and their heirs.

State the title upon O's death. O's estate has a fee simple subject to an executory limitation, and O's descendants living at the time his estate is distributed have a springing executory interest in fee simple.

Does the executory interest violate the Rule Against Perpetuities? Although it would appear impossible for the estate not be distributed in a timely manner, the Rule against Perpetuities is not concerned with practical probabilities, but rather with abstract possibilities. Is it possible, regardless of how unlikely the scenario, that O's estate will not be distributed until after all the lives in being plus 21 years? Put it to the test. Assume that O's executor is A, and that O's descendants then living are X and Y. **Create** a new executor, B, and a new descendant, Z. **Kill** all the lives in being at the time the interests were created: A, X and Y and the rest of the world alive at that time. **Count** 21 years. Is it possible that the new executor may take more than 21 years to complete distribution of O's estate? Yes.[149] Just as with the more traditional executory interest following a fee simple defeasible, **the executory limitation must be tied to a life in being at the time the interest is created.**

2. The Rule against Perpetuities applied to the "future interest only" conveyance.

The classic executory interest is a shifting executory interest following a fee simple defeasible. The executory interest following a "future interest only" conveyance is analogous to the classic executory interest except that in the "future interest only" conveyance the right to possession is being taken from the grantor, not a third party.

For example:

EXAMPLE 12

O →   To A and her heirs if A graduates from law school.

State the title. O has a fee simple subject to an executory limitation, and A has a springing executory interest. A's executory interest will cut short

---

[149] In Wills & Trusts circles this type of conveyance is commonly known as the "slothful executor" problem.

O's fee simple if the express condition precedent occurs (here, if A graduates from law school).

Just as with the classic executory interest, the key to applying the Rule against Perpetuities to the "future interest only" conveyance is whether the express condition is tied to a life in being or not. Where the express condition is tied to a life in being, it will never violate the Rule against Perpetuities. Where the express condition is not tied to a life in being, it almost always violates the Rule against Perpetuities.

Return to the example above. Does A's springing executory interest violate the Rule against Perpetuities? Put it to the test. First, create someone in whom the interest can vest, but only after the lives in being plus 21 years perpetuities period. You cannot. A is the only person who can satisfy the express condition precedent. A must graduate from law school for the executory interest to vest and become possessory. The interest does not violate the Rule against Perpetuities.

Most "future interest only" conveyances will not violate the Rule against Perpetuities because the express condition typically is tied to a life in being. But it need not be. For example:

EXAMPLE 13

O →   To A and her heirs when a woman is elected President
        of the United States.

State the title. O has a fee simple subject to an executory limitation, and A has a springing executory interest in fee simple. A's executory interest is subject to the Rule against Perpetuities. Put it to the test. Create a new person in whom the interest can vest, but only after the lives in being plus 21 years perpetuities period – X, an heir of A. Kill A, O and everyone else. Count 21 years. Is it conceivable that a woman will still not have been elected President of the United States? Yes. Is it conceivable that thereafter a woman will be elected President? Yes. Where the express condition is not tied to a life in being, the executory interest typically will violate the Rule against Perpetuities.

As with classic executory interests, whether an executory interest following a "future interest only" conveyance violates the Rule against Perpetuities usually turns on whether the express condition is tied to a life in being. More often than not, in the "future interest only" conveyance the express condition *will* be tied to a life in being, but you have to read and analyze each conveyance carefully to see whether it violates the Rule against Perpetuities.

3. The Rule against Perpetuities applied to the executory interest following a vested remainder subject to divestment.

In applying the Rule against Perpetuities to executory interests following a vested remainder subject to divestment, the key is whether the divesting condition is one which **must occur, if at all,** during the estate preceding the vested remainder, or whether the divesting condition is one which **may occur** during the estate preceding the vested remainder. The vested remainder subject to divestment almost invariably follows a life estate.[150] If the divesting condition **must occur, if at all,** during the life estate, then the executory interest will become possessory, not the vested remainder. Notice what that means. The executory interest must become possessory, if at all, either during or upon the expiration of the life estate. Thus where the vested remainder subject to divestment follows a life estate, and the divesting condition **must occur, if at all,** during or upon expiration of the life estate, the executory interest cannot violate the Rule against Perpetuities.

The following example demonstrates that point:

EXAMPLE 14

O →   To A for life, then to B and his heirs, but if A sells
         alcohol on the land, then to C and her heirs.

---

[150] In theory, the vested remainder subject to divestment could follow a fee tail, in which case there could be a potential Rule against Perpetuities problem, but because the fee tail has practically been abolished and even at common law such a conveyance was extremely rare, those scenarios are beyond the scope of this material. The qualifications in this paragraph, then, pertain to these scenarios which are beyond the scope of this material, and as applied to the norm (the vested remainder subject to divestment following a life estate), there is no Rule against Perpetuities problem.

State the title. A has a life estate. B has a vested remainder in fee simple subject to divestment, and C has a shifting executory interest in fee simple.

C's shifting executory interest is subject to the Rule against Perpetuities. Put it to the test. **Create** an heir for B, X, and an heir for C, Y. **Kill** all the lives in being at the time the executory interest was created: A, B, and C. The problem is that the divesting condition is tied to the life tenant. Thus, the executory interest must become possessory, if at all, during or at the expiration of the life estate. It is impossible to delay the vesting until after the lives in being plus 21 years. Thus, the Rule against Perpetuities is not really a problem for executory interests following a vested remainder subject to divestment where the divesting condition is one which **must occur, if at all,** during the preceding life estate.[151]

On the other hand, if the divesting condition is one which **may** occur during the preceding estate, but may not occur until after the vested remainder has become possessory, for purposes of the Rule against Perpetuities, this scenario is analogous to the fee simple subject to an executory limitation scenario. Unless the divesting condition is tied to a life in being, the executory interest will violate the Rule against Perpetuities and will be void.

4.   The Rule against Perpetuities applied to the executory interest following the "gap" scenario.

Although one might think that the Rule against Perpetuities does not have much application to the "gap" scenario, the "gap" scenario is much like the executory interest where the grantor's possessory estate is cut short and for that reason may be deceptively tricky. To the extent the "gap" is tied solely to an express time period less than 21 years, the Rule against Perpetuities will not be a problem. To the extent the "gap" is tied to the occurrence of an event, the Rule is very applicable.

The Rule typically is not a problem where the "gap" is solely an express time period less than 21 years. For example:

---

[151] If, however, the underlying finite estate is a term of years greater than 21 years, or a fee tail, the Rule against Perpetuities is very much a problem for executory interests which follow a vested remainder subject to divestment.

EXAMPLE 15

O → to A for life, then 1 year after A's death, to B and his heirs.

State the title. A has a life estate, O has a reversion in fee simple subject to an executory limitation, and B has a springing executory interest in fee simple.

B's executory interest is subject to the Rule against Perpetuities. Put it to the test. **Create** a new life in being who will be eligible to claim possession of the property under the interest being tested - X, an heir for B (we also need an heir for O, Y). **Kill** all the lives in being at the time the executory interest was created: O, A and **B. Count** 21 years. Is it possible that the executory interest will become possessory but only **after** the lives in being plus 21 years? No. The executory interest must become possessory one year after the killing of the lives in being. There is no way to delay the vesting. Thus, where the "gap" is tied **solely** to an express time period that is less than 21 years, there is no Rule against Perpetuities problem and the interest is valid.

On the other hand, where the "gap" is tied to an event, if the occurrence can be delayed there will be Rule against Perpetuities problems. For example:

EXAMPLE 16

O → To A for life, then 1 year after the election of a Libertarian President of the United States, to B and his heirs.

State the title. A has a life estate, O has a reversion in fee simple subject to an executory limitation, and B has a springing executory interest in fee simple.

B's executory interest is subject to the Rule against Perpetuities. The scenario here is much like the scenario discussed above where the grantor's possessory estate is being cut short with the future interest being in a third party. If the occurrence is not tied to a life in being, there is going to be a Rule against Perpetuities problem. Put the above example to the test.

Create the necessary new lives in being: an heir for O and an heir for B. **Kill** all the lives in being at the time the interest was created: O, A and B. **Count** 21 years. Is it possible that the executory interest will still not be possessory? Yes. Is it possible that thereafter a Libertarian could be elected President of the United States? Yes. Therefore, the executory interest violates the Rule against Perpetuities and is void.

THE RULE AGAINST PERPETUITIES EXECUTORY INTERESTS
PROBLEM SET – PROBLEM SET 14

For each of the following problems, (1) state the title of the conveyance as drafted, (2) state if any of the interests are subject to the Rule against Perpetuities, and (3) state if the interest violates the Rule.

1.   O → To A and her heirs as long as the land is used for educational purposes; and if it is not used for educational purposes, then to B and her heirs.

2.   O → to whoever is the President of Pepperdine University at the time of distribution of my estate and his or her heirs.

3.   O → To A for life, then to B and her heirs, but if B ever sells liquor on the land, to C and her heirs.

C. CLASS GIFTS

As discussed above, conveyances to a class of people create unique challenges when determining whether a remainder is contingent or vested. With respect to class conveyances, there is a third category: vested subject to open. Vested subject to open is like being partially vested. You might think that the same would be true with respect to the Rule against Perpetuities: the conveyance to the class could be valid, invalid, or partially valid/invalid. That is not the case. The whole class, every single possible member of the class **must** vest within the lives in being or the **whole** class conveyance is invalid. **If you can create one scenario where one class member vests, but only after the lives in being plus 21 years after the creation of the conveyance to the class, the interest is void.**

Remainders to a class are typically contingent because not all members of the class are born and thus more members of the class may enter. A class can **also** be contingent because of an express condition precedent. For purposes of the Rule against Perpetuities, the class must close, and if there is an express condition precedent, all members of the class must satisfy the condition precedent, within the lives in being plus 21 years.

Where there is no express condition precedent, there is only one class gift after the life estate, and the identified class does not skip a generation, there is no Rule against Perpetuities problem. For example:

EXAMPLE 17

O →   To A for life, then to A's children and their heirs.

State the title. A has a life estate, A's children have a contingent remainder in fee simple, and O has a reversion in fee simple.

The contingent remainder in A's children is subject to the Rule against Perpetuities. But because the class will close upon A's death and there is no express condition precedent, there is no Rule against Perpetuities problem. The remainder will vest, if at all, completely upon A's death. There is no scenario which would delay the vesting until **after** the lives in being plus 21 years. The same would be true if the contingent remainder were in B's children, or anybody's children. The same would be true if the interest were in A's descendants or A's issue. As long as there is only one class remainder, there is no express condition precedent, and the description of the class is one which does not skip a generation, the class remainder will not violate the Rule against Perpetuities because it must vest, if at all, upon the expiration of the life estate (and it cannot be delayed until after the lives in being plus 21 years).

If however, there is only one class remainder, there is no express condition precedent, but the description of the class skips a generation, the class interest will violate the Rule against Perpetuities. Return to the example above and modify it slightly:

EXAMPLE 18

O → To A for life, then to A's grandchildren and their heirs.

State the title. A has a life estate, A's grandchildren have a contingent remainder in fee simple, and O has a reversion in fee simple.

The remainder in A's grandchildren, be it contingent or vested subject to open, is subject to the Rule against Perpetuities. Put is to the test. Create someone who will be eligible to claim possession of the property under the interest but after the lives in being plus 21 years, so create as far back in the chain as possible: create a new child for A, child X. **Kill** all the lives in being at the time the interest was created: O, A, all of A's children alive at the time of the conveyance, if any, and all of A's grandchildren alive at the time of the conveyance, if any. **Count** 21 years. Is it possible that thereafter X will have a child, Y, a grandchild of A, who would be able to claim possession of the property pursuant to the remainder?[152] Yes. Thus the remainder in A's grandchildren, be it contingent or vested subject to open, is invalid. **Where there is only one class remainder and no express condition precedent, but the description of the class skips a generation, the remainder will violate the Rule against Perpetuities.**

---

[152] Remember, for analytical purposes, the Rule against Perpetuities ignores the destructibility of contingent remainders doctrine.

The trickier problems develop when either (1) there are stacked contingent or vested subject to open remainders, and/or (2) there is an express condition precedent on the class. Start with the former first:

EXAMPLE 19

O →   To A for life, then to B's children for life, then to B's grandchildren and their heirs.

Assume A and B are alive, that B has 4 children (K, L, M, and N) and 2 grandchildren (R and S).

State the title.   A has a life estate, B's children have a vested remainder subject to open in life estate, and B's grandchildren have a vested remainder subject to open in fee simple.   There are two remainders which are subject to the Rule against Perpetuities.   Notice even if one or both of them were contingent remainders, they would still be subject to the Rule against Perpetuities.   The analysis would be the same.   But the example involves a vested subject to open because it was assumed that you would probably be more inclined to find these valid than contingent remainders.   But even with the vested subject to open, you have to put it to the test.

First, test the vested remainder subject to open in B's children. **Create** a new being who would be eligible to claim the interest in question: another child for B, X.   Kill all the lives in being at the time the first remainder was created: O, A, B, K, L, M, N, R and S.   **Count** 21 years.   Is it possible that X's remainder will vest but **only** after the lives in being plus 21 years?   No.   X's interest will vest, if at all, only upon the killing of the lives in being, not after the additional 21 years.   There is no Rule against Perpetuities problem with the first remainder (which is consistent with the observation above that when there is only one remainder with no express condition precedent, there is no Rule against Perpetuities problem).

When there is no express condition precedent, but stacked contingent or vested subject to open remainders, the Rule against Perpetuities problem is with the second contingent or vested subject to open remainder.   Returning to the example above, test the vested remainder subject to open in B's grandchildren. **Create** as far back in the process as possible, so create a new child for B, child X, and a new grandchild for B, grandchild Y. **Kill** all the lives in being at the time the first remainder was created: O, A, B, K, L, M, N, R and S. **Count** 21 years. Is it possible that thereafter X will die, thereby closing the class of B's grandchildren and making the interest possessory in Y? Certainly. Thus, because we created a scenario in which the vested remainder subject to open became possessory in a class member after the lives in being plus 21 years, the class gift is void. **Whenever there is no express condition precedent but there are contingent or vested subject to open conveyances which are stacked, the second contingent or vested subject to open invariably will be void.**

The other class gift scenario that has potential Rule against Perpetuities problems is a remainder to a class which contains an express condition precedent which can take more than 21 years to satisfy. For example:

EXAMPLE 20

O →   To A for life, then to B's children who reach age 30 and their heirs.

Assume A and B are alive, and B has 4 children (F, age 39, G, age 36, H, age 33, and I, age 31).

State the title. A has a life estate, and B's children who reach the age of 30 have a vested remainder subject to open in fee simple.

Why is the remainder vested subject to open if all of B's children are over the age of 30? Because B can have more children. What if B were an 85 year old woman? Putting aside the advances in reproductive technology and techniques, the common law presumed each individual was fertile until death.[153] Put the interest to the test. Create a new being who could claim the property under the interest being challenged - a new child for B, X.

---

[153] In Wills & Trusts circles, this possibility is commonly known as the "fertile octogenarian." The fertile octogenarian often creates Rule against Perpetuities problems.

Kill all the lives in being at the time the interest was created: O, A, B, F, G, H, and I. Notice this closes the class but does not fully vest the class because X has not satisfied the express condition precedent. **Count** 21 years. Is it possible that X could live another 9 years, thereby satisfying the express condition precedent and being able to claim possession of the property? Yes. Thus the vested remainder subject to open in B's children who reach the age of 30 is void.

If the express condition precedent for the class is one which must be satisfied, if at all, within 21 years, then there is no Rule against Perpetuities problem. Modify the above example just slightly:

EXAMPLE 21

O →   To A for life, then to B's children who reach age 21 and their heirs.

Assume A and B are alive, that B has 4 children (F, age 39, G, age 36, H, age 33, and I, age 31).

State the title. A has a life estate, and B's children who reach the age of 21 have a vested remainder subject to open in fee simple.

Again, the vested remainder subject to open in the children of B who reach age 21 is subject to the Rule against Perpetuities. Put the interest to the test. Create a new being who could claim the property under the interest being challenged - a new child for B, X. Kill all the lives in being at the time the interest was created: O, A, B, F, G, H, and I. Notice this closes the class but does not fully vest the class because X has not satisfied the express condition precedent. **Count** 21 years. Is it possible that X could satisfying the express condition precedent and be able to claim possession of the property but not until **after** the running of the 21 years? No, X will have to turn 21 before the 21 years has fully run. Because the express condition is one which must be satisfied, if at all, within 21 years, it cannot violate the Rule against Perpetuities.

THE RULE AGAINST PERPETUITIES CLASS GIFTS PROBLEM SET – PROBLEM SET 15

For each of the following problems, (1) state the title of the conveyance as drafted, (2) state if any of the interests are subject to the Rule against Perpetuities, and (3) state if the interest violates the Rule. (Treat the sub parts under each conveyance as cumulative factual developments.)

1.   O →   To A for life, then to A's children and their heirs.

   a)   assume A has no children.

   b)   assume A has a child, X.

   c)   assume A dies.

2.   O →   to A for life, then to B's children and their heirs.

   a)   assume B has no children.

   b)   assume B has a child, X.

c)   assume A dies.

d)   assume B has a child, Y.

3.   O → To A for life, then to A's grandchildren and their heirs.

A has no grandchildren yet.

4.   O → To A for life, then to A's children who reach age 21 and his or her heirs.

Assume A has 2 children: X, age 25; and Y, age 5.

5.   O → To A for life, then to B's children who reach age 25 and his or her heirs.

Assume B has a child, X, age 27.

Appendix A

ANSWERS TO PROBLEM SETS

ANSWERS TO PROBLEM SET 1

1.   O →   To A and his children.

    (a)   Common law: **No fee simple absolute. Improper words of limitation.**

    (b)   Modern trend: **Unclear, but probably a fee simple absolute. The presumption would be that the grantor used the word "children" to indicate that A should get the property, and upon his death, that it should go to his children, his heirs apparent. That intent is consistent with the fee simple absolute.**

2.   O →   To A and his heirs.

    (a)   Common law: **A fee simple absolute is conveyed - proper words of limitation.**

    (b)   Modern trend: **A fee simple absolute is conveyed. The modern trend is a more lenient standard, so any language that would convey a fee simple absolute under the common law approach should do the same under the modern trend (absent evidence of a contrary intent despite the proper terminology).**

3.   O →   To A in fee simple absolute.

    (a)   Common law: **No fee simple absolute. Improper words of limitation. The common law approach is very strict, insisting on proper words of limitation as opposed to focusing on intent.**

(b) Modern trend: **A fee simple absolute is conveyed. The modern trend focuses on the grantor's intent. Here, the grantor clearly intends to convey a fee simple absolute even though he or she did not use the traditional words of limitation.**

4.   O →   To the heirs of A.

(a) Common law: **No fee simple absolute. Improper words of limitation.**

(b) Modern trend: **Unclear; unlikely to convey a fee simple absolute. You have not covered enough material to see all the ambiguities inherent in the language of this conveyance. The biggest problem to finding that this conveys a fee simple absolute to A is that the words of purchase technically give the property to the heirs of A, not A. But the court may take extrinsic evidence to try to resolve the ambiguity. If the only evidence, however, were the language of the conveyance, this arguably is not enough to convey a fee simple absolute under the modern trend.**

5.   O →   To B.

(a) Common law: **No fee simple absolute. Improper words of limitation. (You will learn later that this language would convey the property to B for the duration of his or her life – a life estate.)**

(b) Modern trend: **A fee simple absolute is conveyed. Absent extrinsic evidence to the contrary, the presumption would be that the grantor intended to convey all that he or she had to the grantee. Because there are no words limiting what the grantee is to take, assuming the grantor held a fee simple absolute, the grantee would take a fee simple absolute.**

6.   O → All to A.

   (a) Common law: **No fee simple absolute. Improper words of limitation. The common law approach is very strict, insisting on proper words of limitation as opposed to focusing on intent.**

   (b) Modern trend: **Fee simple absolute. Absent extrinsic evidence to the contrary, the presumption would be that the grantor intended to convey all that he or she had to the grantee. Because there are no words limiting what the grantee is to take, assuming the grantor held a fee simple absolute, the grantee would take all a fee simple absolute.**

7.   O → To A forever.

   (a) Common law: **No fee simple absolute. Improper words of limitation. The common law approach is very strict, insisting on proper words of limitation as opposed to focusing on intent.**

   (b) Modern trend: **A fee simple absolute is conveyed. The modern trend focuses on the grantor's intent. Here, the grantor clearly intends to convey a fee simple absolute even though he or she did not use the traditional words of limitation.**

ANSWERS TO PROBLEM SET 2

1.   O → To A and her heirs as long as she uses the land for educational purposes.

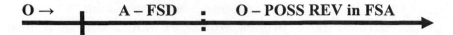

A has a Fee Simple Determinable, and
O has a possibility of Reverter.

2.   O → To A and her heirs, but if she stops using the land for educational purposes, then O has the right to re-enter and re-claim the land.

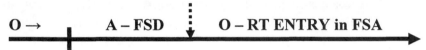

A has a Fee Simple Subject to a Condition Subsequent, and
O has a Right of Entry/power of termination.

3.   O → To A and her heirs as long as she does not re-marry, then to B and his heirs.

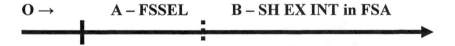

A has a Fee Simple Subject to an Executory Limitation, and
B has a Shifting Executory Interest in Fee Simple.

4.   O → To A and her heirs, but if A remarries, then to B and his heirs.

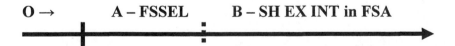

A has a Fee Simple Subject to an Executory Limitation, and
B has a Shifting Executory Interest in Fee Simple.

5.   O →   To A and her heirs if she graduates from law school.

     O →   **A – Sp EX INT in FSA**

O has a Fee Simple Subject to an Executory Limitation, and A has a Springing Executory Interest in Fee Simple.

(This will be covered in more detail in Chapter 6, so do not worry if you did not get this one. This was intended to get you thinking about this conveyance more than to test your understanding at this point.)

ANSWERS TO PROBLEM SET 3

1.   O →   To A for life, then to B and her heirs.

   **A has a LIFE ESTATE, and
   B has a REMAINDER in fee simple absolute.**

2.   O →   To A for life.

   **A has a LIFE ESTATE, and
   O has a REVERSION in fee simple absolute.**

3.   O →   To A and the heirs of her body, then to B and her heirs.

   **A has a FEE TAIL, and
   B has a REMAINDER in fee simple absolute.**

4.   O →   To A and the heirs of her body.

   **A has a FEE TAIL, and
   O has a REVERSION in fee simple absolute.**

5.   O →   To A and her heirs as long as she farms the land organically.

   **A has a FEE SIMPLE DETERMINABLE, and
   O has a POSSIBILITY OF REVERTER in fee simple absolute.**

6.   O →   To A, then to B, and then to C and her heirs.

   (a) Common law: **A has a LIFE ESTATE, B HAS A REMAINDER in LIFE ESTATE, and C has a REMAINDER in FEE SIMPLE ABSOLUTE .**

   (b) Modern Trend: **Same.** Although A and B may try to argue that they have a fee simple, O's use of proper terminology to describe C's interest shows that O knew what he or she was doing.

7.   O →   To A for 99 years.

   A has a TERM OF YEARS, and

O has a REVERSION in fee simple absolute.

8.　O →　To A and her heirs, then to B and her heirs.

**A has a FEE SIMPLE ABSOLUTE, and
B has a NOTHING in fee simple absolute.**

9.　O →　To A in fee simple.

　　(a)　Common law: **A has a LIFE ESTATE, and O has a REVERSION in FEE SIMPLE ABSOLUTE.**
　　(b)　Modern trend:　**A has a FEE SIMPLE ABSOLUTE.**

10.　O →　To A.

　　(a)　Common law: **A has a LIFE ESTATE, and O has a REVERSION in FEE SIMPLE ABSOLUTE.**
　　(b)　Modern trend:　**A has a FEE SIMPLE ABSOLUTE.**

11.　O →　To A for ever and ever.

　　(a)　Common law: **A has a LIFE ESTATE, and O has a REVERSION in FEE SIMPLE ABSOLUTE.**
　　(b)　Modern trend:　**A has a FEE SIMPLE ABSOLUTE.**

12.　O →　To A and her heirs, but if A hunts wildlife on the land, then to B and his heirs.

**A has a FEE SIMPLE SUBJECT TO AN EXECUTORY LIMITATION, and
B has a SHIFTING EXECUTORY INTEREST in FEE SIMPLE.**

13. .　O →　To A for life, then to B and her heirs.
　　　　Thereafter, A transfers her interest to C.

**C has a LIFE ESTATE PUR AUTRE VIE (measured by A's life), and
B has a REMAINDER in FEE SIMPLE ABSOLUTE.**

ANSWERS TO PROBLEM SET 4

1.   O →   To A for life, then to B and her heirs.

   A has a LIFE ESTATE,
   B has a VESTED REMAINDER in FEE SIMPLE ABSOLUTE,
   O has NOTHING.

2.   O →   To A for life, then to B and the heirs of her body, then to C and his heirs.

   A has a LIFE ESTATE,
   B has a VESTED REMAINDER in FEE TAIL,
   C has a VESTED REMAINDER in FEE SIMPLE ABSOLUTE,
   O has NOTHING.

3.   O →   To A and the heirs of her body, then to B for life, then to C and her heirs as long as maintains the wetlands on the property.

   A has a FEE TAIL,
   B has a VESTED REMAINDER in LIFE ESTATE,
   C has a VESTED REMAINDER in FEE SIMPLE
   **   DETERMINABLE,**
   O has a POSSIBILITY OF REVERTER in FEE SIMPLE
   **   ABSOLUTE.**

4.   O →   To A for life, then to B for life, then to C for life.

   A has a LIFE ESTATE,
   B has a VESTED REMAINDER in LIFE ESTATE,
   C has a VESTED REMINDER in LIFE ESTATE,
   O has a REVERSION in FEE SIMPLE ABSOLUTE.

5.   O →   To A for 10 years, then to B and the heirs of her body, then to C for life.

   A has a TERM OF YEARS,
   B has a VESTED REMAINDER in FEE TAIL,
   C has a VESTED REMAINDER in LIFE ESTATE,

O has a REVERSION in FEE SIMPLE ABSOLUTE.

6.   O → To A for life, then to O and his heirs.

A has a LIFE ESTATE,
O has a REVERSION in FEE SIMPLE ABSOLUTE.

7.   To A and the heirs of her body, then to B and the heirs of his body, then to C and her heirs, but if she begins to develop the property, then O has the right to re-enter and reclaim the property.

A has a FEE TAIL,
B has a VESTED REMAINDER in FEE TAIL,
C has a VESTED REMAINDER in FEE SIMPLE SUBJECT TO
     CONDITION SUBSEQUENT,
O has a RIGHT OF ENTRY/POWER OF TERMINATION in
     FEE SIMPLE ABSOLUTE.

8.   O →   To A for life, then to B and her heirs as long as she farms the land, then to C and her heirs.

A has a LIFE ESTATE,
B has a VESTED REMAINDER in FEE SIMPLE SUBJECT TO
     AN EXECUTORY LIMITATION,
C has a SHIFTING EXECUTORY INTEREST in FEE SIMPLE
     ABSOLUTE.

ANSWERS TO PROBLEM SET 5

1.   O →   A.

**A has A LIFE ESTATE,
O has a REVERSION in FEE SIMPLE ABSOLUTE.**

2.   O →   A and her heirs.

**A has a FEE SIMPEL ABSOLUTE,
O has NOTHING.**

3.   O →   A for life.

**A has a LIFE ESTATE,
O has a REVERSION in FEE SIMPLE ABSOLUTE.**

4.   O →   A and her heirs as long as the land is never used for commercial purposes.

**A has a FEE SIMPLE DETERMINABLE,
O has a POSSIBILITY OF REVERTER in FEE SIMPLE ABSOLUTE.**

5.   O →   A and her heirs, but if the land is ever used for commercial purposes, then O and his heirs shall have the right to reenter and reclaim the land.

**A has a FEE SIMPLE SUBJECT TO A CONDITION
    SUBSEQUENT,
O has a RIGHT OF ENTRY/POWER OF TERMINATION in
    FEE SIMPLE ABSOLUTE.**

6.   O →   A and the heirs of her body.

**A has A FEE TAIL,
O has a REVERSION in FEE SIMPLE ABSOLUTE.**

7. O → A and her heirs as long as A uses the land for agricultural purposes, then to B and his heirs.

    A has a **FEE SIMPLE DETERMINABLE,**
    B has a **SHIFTING EXECUTORY INTEREST in FEE SIMPLE ABSOLUTE.**

8. O → A and her heirs, but if A goes surfing, then to B and his heirs.

    A has a **FEE SIMPLE SUBJECT TO AN EXECUTORY LIMITATION,**
    B has **A SHIFTING EXECUTORY INTEREST in FEE SIMPLE ABSOLUTE.**

9. O → A and the heirs of her body, then to B and his heirs.

    A has a **FEE TAIL,**
    B has a **VESTED REMAINDER in FEE SIMPLE ABSOLUTE, and**
    O has **NOTHING.**

10. O → A and the heirs of her body, then if B is still living, to B and his heirs.

    A has a **FEE TAIL,**
    B has a **CONTINGENT REMAINDER in FEE SIMPLE ABSOLUTE, and**
    O has a **REVERSION in FEE SIMPLE ABSOLUTE.**

11. O → A and her children.

    (a) Common law: **The only thing certain is that A does not have a fee simple absolute. Depending on the grantor's intent and how the courts construed the poorly drafted instrument, A could either have a life estate all alone, with O having a reversion in fee simple absolute; or A and her children have a joint life estate with O having a reversion in fee simple absolute.**

(b)   Modern trend: **A and her children could hold title concurrently (joint tenants or tenants in common – common law vs. modern trend) in fee simple.**

12.   O →   A for life, then to B and his heirs.

A has a LIFE ESTATE,
B has a VESTED REMAINDER in FEE SIMPLE ABSOLUTE.
O has NOTHING.

13.   O →   A for life, then to B and his heirs if B marries C, and if B does not, to D and his heirs.

A has A LIFE ESTATE,
B has a CONTINGENT REMAINDER in FEE SIMPLE
    ABSOLUTE,
D has an ALTERNATIVE CONTINGENT REMAINDER IN
    FEE SIMPLE ABSOLUTE, and
O HAS A REVERSION in FEE SIMPLE ABSOLUTE.

14.   O →   A for life, then to B and his heirs if B returns from London.

A has a LIFE ESTATE,
B has a CONTINGENT REMAINDER in FEE SIMPLE
    ABSOLUTE,
O has a REVERSION in FEE SIMPLE ABSOLUTE.

15.   O →   A for life, then to the person who is then Dean of the Law School and his or her heirs.

A has a LIFE ESTATE,
THE DEAN has a CONTINGENT REMAINDER in FEE
    SIMPLE ABSOLUTE, and
O has a REVERSION in FEE SIMPLE ABSOLUTE.

16.   O →   A for life, then to B for life, then to C's heirs and their heirs. Assume C is still alive.

A has a LIFE ESTATE,

B has a VESTED REMAINDER in LFE ESTATE,
C's HEIRS have a CONTINGENT REMAINDER[154] **in FEE**
     SIMPLE ABSOLUTE, and
O has a REVERSION in FEE SIMPLE ABSOLUTE.

17.   O →   A for life, then to B and his heirs as long as the land is farmed.

A has a LIFE ESTATE,
B has a VESTED REMAINDER in FEE SIMPLE
     DETERMINABLE, and
O has a POSSIBILITY OF REVERTER in FEE SIMPLE
     ABSOLUTE.

18.   O →   A for life, then if B has agreed to farm the land, to B and his heirs.

A has a LIFE ESTATE,
B has a CONTINGENT REMAINDER in FEE SIMPLE
     ABSOLUTE, and
O has a REVERSION in FEE SIMPLE ABSOLUTE.

19.   O →   A for life, then to B and his heirs if B marries C.

A has a LIFE ESTATE,
B has a CONTINGENT REMAINDER in FEE SIMPLE
     ABSOLUTE, and
O has a REVERSION in FEE SIMPLE ABSOLUTE.

20.   O →   A for life, then to B and his heirs if B attends A's wedding.

A has a LIFE ESTATE,
B has a CONTINGENT REMAINDER in FEE SIMPLE
     ABSOLUTE, and
O has a REVERSION in FEE SIMPLE ABSOLUTE.

---

[154] A person does not have heirs until he or she dies, only apparent heirs. To qualify as an heir you have to survive the decedent. Thus C's heirs are not ascertainable while C is still alive.

ANSWERS TO PROBLEM SET 6

1.   O →   To A for life, then to B and her heirs as long as the land is
             farmed.

   A: **has a LIFE ESTATE**
   B: **has a VESTED REMAINDER in FEE SIMPLE**
             DETERMINABLE
   O: **has a POSSIBILITY OF REVERTER in FEE SIMPLE**
             ABSOLUTE.

2.   O →   To A for life, then to B and her heirs, but if B stops farming the
             land, then O can re-enter and reclaim the land.

   A: **has a LIFE ESTATE**
   B: **has a VESTED REMAINDER in FEE SIMPLE SUBJECT**
             TO A CONDITION SUBSEQUENT
   O: **has a RIGHT OF ENTRY/POWER OF TERMINATION**
             in FEE SIMPLE ABSOLUTE.

3.   O →   To A for life, then to B and her heirs as long as the land is
             farmed, then to C and her heirs.

   A: **has a LIFE ESTATE**
   B: **has a VESTED REMAINDER in FEE SIMPLE SUBJECT**
             TO AN EXECUTORY LIMITATION
   C: **has a SHIFTING EXECUTORY INTEREST in FEE**
             SIMPLE ABSOLUTE.

4.   O →   To A for life, then to B and her heirs, but if B stops farming the
             land, then to C and her heirs.

   A: **has a LIFE ESTATE**
   B: **has a VESTED REMAINDER in FEE SIMPLE SUBJECT**
             TO AN EXECUTORY LIMITATION
   C: **has a SHIFTING EXECUTORY INTEREST in FEE**
             SIMPLE ABSOLUTE.

5.   O →   To A for life, then to B and her heirs, then to C and her heirs.

  A: **has a LIFE ESTATE**
  B: **has a VESTED REMAINDER in FEE SIMPLE.**
  C: **Nothing. (Once O conveyed an unqualified fee simple to B, O had nothing left to give to C. Even under the modern trend, where C can argue that O arguably intended to give C an interest, it is unlikely that a court would give C an interest. There is no express condition indicating when B's fee simple is to be cut.)**

6.   O →   To A for life, then to B and her heirs, but if B sells alcohol on the land, then to X and her heirs.

 (a) Assume A, B and X are alive.

  A: **has a LIFE ESTATE**
  B: **has a VESTED REMAINDER in FEE SIMPLE SUBJECT TO AN EXECUTORY LIMITATION**
  X: **has a SHIFTING EXECUTORY INTEREST in FEE SIMPLE ABSOLUTE.**

 (b) Assume A dies and B and X are alive.

  B: **has a FEE SIMPLE SUBJECT TO AN EXECUTORY LIMITATION**
  X: **has a SHIFTING EXECUTORY INTEREST in FEE SIMPLE ABSOLUTE.**

7.   O →   To A for life, then to B and her heirs if B graduates from law school.

 (a) Assume A and B are both alive and B has not graduated from law school yet.

  A: **has a LIFE ESTATE**
  B: **has a CONTINGENT REMAINDER in FEE SIMPLE ABSOLUTE**
  O: **has a REVERSION IN FEE SIMPLE ABSOLUTE.**

8.   O →   To A and her heirs if A graduates from medical school.

     O: **has a FEE SIMPLE SUBJECT TO AN EXECUTORY LIMITATION**

     A: **has a SPRINGING EXECUTORY INTEREST in FEE SIMPLE ABSOLUTE.**

ANSWERS TO PROBLEM SET 7

1. O → To A for life, then to B and her heirs as long as the land is farmed.

    A: **has a LIFE ESTATE**
    B: **has a VESTED REMAINDER in FEE SIMPLE DETERMINABLE**
    O: **has a POSSIBIILTY OF REVERTER in FEE SIMPLE ABSOLUTE.**

2. O → To A for life, then to B and her heirs, but if B stops farming the land, then O can re-enter and reclaim the land.

    A: **has a LIFE ESTATE**
    B: **has a VESTED REMAINDER in FEE SIMPLE SUBJECT TO A CONDITION SUBSEQUENT**
    O: **has a RIGHT OF ENTRY/POWER OF TERMINATION in FEE SIMPLE ABSOLUTE.**

3. O → To A for life, then to B and her heirs as long as the land is farmed, then to C and her heirs.

    A: **has a LIFE ESTATE**
    B: **has a VESTED REMAINDER in FEE SIMPLE SUBJECT TO AN EXECUTORY LIMITATION**
    C: **has a SHIFTING EXECUTORY INTEREST in FEE SIMPLE ABSOLUTE.**

4. O → To A for life, then to B and her heirs, but if B stops farming the land, then to C and her heirs.

    A: **has a LIFE ESTATE**
    B: **has a VESTED REMAINDER in FEE SIMPLE SUBJECT TO AN EXECUTORY LIMITATION**
    C: **has a SHIFTING EXECUTORY INTEREST in FEE SIMPLE ABSOLUTE.**

5.   O →   To A for life, then to B and her heirs, but if A stops farming the land, then to C and her heirs.

    A: **has a LIFE ESTATE**[155]
    B: **has a VESTED REMAINDER, SUBJECT TO DIVESTMENT, in FEE SIMPLE ABSOLUTE**
    C: **has a SHIFTING EXECUTORY INTERST in FEE SIMPLE ABSOLUTE.**

6.   O →   To A for life, then to B and her heirs, but if B marries C, then to X and her heirs.

    (a) Assume A, B, C and X are alive.

    A: **has a LIFE ESTATE**[156]
    B: **has a VESTED REMAINDER, SUBJECT TO DIVESTMENT, in FEE SIMPLE**
    X: **has a SHIFTING EXECUTORY INTERST in FEE SIMPLE ABSOLUTE.**

    (b) Assume A dies and B, C and X are alive.

    A: **has a FEE SIMPLE SUBJECT TO AN EXECUTORY LIMITATION**
    X: **has a SHIFTING EXECUTORY INTEREST in FEE SIMPLE ABSOLUTE.**

7.   O →   To A for life, then to B and her heirs if B graduates from law school.

    Assume A and B are both alive and B has not graduated from law school yet.

    A: **has a LIFE ESTATE**
    B: **has a CONTINGENT REMAINDER in FEE SIMPLE ABSOLUTE**
    O: **has a REVERSION IN FEE SIMPLE ABSOLUTE.**

---

[155] Whether the divesting condition would also cut short the life estate is beyond the scope of this introductory coverage.
[156] *Id.*.

8.   O →   To A for life, then to B and her heirs, but if A fails to graduate
            from law school, then to C and her heirs.

      A: **has a LIFE ESTATE**[157]
      B: **has a VESTED REMAINDER, SUBJECT TO**
            DIVESTMENT, in FEE SIMPLE ABSOLUTE
      C: **has a SHIFTING EXECUTORY INTERSST in FEE**
            SIMPLE ABSOLUTE.

9.   O →   To A for life, then to B and her heirs if A graduates from law
            school, but if A fails to graduate from law school, then to C
            and her heirs.

      A: **has a LIFE ESTATE**
      B: **has a CONTINGENT REMAINDER in FEE SIMPLE**
            ABSOLUTE
      C: **has an ALTERNATIVE CONTINGENT REMAINDER IN**
            FEE SIMPLE ABSOLUTE
      O: **has a REVERSION IN FEE SIMPLE ABSOLUTE.**

10.   O →   To A for life, then to B and her heirs as long as B farms the
            land.

      A: **has a LIFE ESTATE**
      B: **has a VESTED REMAINDER in FEE SIMPLE**
            DETERMINABLE
      O: **has a POSSIBILITY OF REVERTER in FEE SIMPLE**
            ABSOLUTE.

11.   O →   To A for life, then to B and her heirs, but if C returns from
            England, then to C and her heirs.

      A: **has a LIFE ESTATE**[158]
      B: **has a VESTED REMAINDER, SUBJECT TO**
            DIVESTMENT, in FEE SIMPLE ABSOLUTE

---

[157] Whether the diverting condition would also cut short the life estate is beyond the scope of this introductory coverage.

[158] *Id.*

C: has a SHIFTING EXECUTORY INTEREST in FEE
        SIMPLE ABSOLUTE.

ANSWERS TO PROBLEM SET 8

1. O → To A for life, then to B and her heirs if B attends A's funeral.

    A: **has a LIFE ESTATE**
    O: **has a REVERSION IN FEE SIMPLE SUBJECT TO AN EXECUTORY LIMITATION**
    B: **has a SPRINGING EXECUTORY INTERST in FEE SIMPLE ABSOLUTE.**

2. O → To A for life, then to B and her heirs if B graduates from law school.

    Assume A has died and B has not graduated from law school yet.

    O: **has a FEE SIMPLE ABSOLUTE (B had a contingent remainder in fee simple absolute which did not vest by the end of the preceding life estate so it was destroyed by operation of law).**

3. O → To A and her heirs as long as the land is farmed, then to B and her heirs

    A: **has a FEE SIMPLE SUBJECT TO AN EXECUTORY LIMITATION**
    B: **has a SHIFTING EXECUTORY INTERST in FEE SIMPLE ABSOLUTE.**

4. O → To A and her heirs, but if the land is used for commercial purposes, then to B and her heirs.

    A: **has a FEE SIMPLE SUBJECT TO AN EXECUTORY LIMITATION**
    B: **has a SHIFTING EXECUTORY INTERST in FEE SIMPLE ABSOLUTE.**

5.   O →   To A and her heirs if she graduates from law school.

        O: **has a FEE SIMPLE SUBJECT TO AN EXECUTORY LIMITATION**

        A: **has a SPRINGING EXECUTORY INTERST in FEE SIMPLE ABSOLUTE.**

6.   O →   To A for life, then after A's funeral, to B and her heirs.

        A: **has a LIFE ESTATE**

        O: **has a REVERSION IN FEE SIMPLE SUBJECT TO AN EXECUTORY LIMITATION.**

        B: **has a SPRINGING EXECUTORY INTEREST in FEE SIMPLE ABSOLUTE.**

7.   O →   To A for life, then to B and his heirs, but if B and his heirs ever use the land for commercial purposes, then to C and her heirs.

        A: **has a LIFE ESTATE**

        B: **has a VESTED REMAINDER in FEE SIMPLE SUBJECT TO AN EXECUTORY LIMITATION**

        C: **has a SHIFTING EXECUTORY INTEREST in FEE SIMPLE ABSOLUTE.**

8.   O →   To A for life, then to B and his heirs, but if A and her heirs ever use the land for commercial purposes, then to C and her heirs.

        A: **has a LIFE ESTATE[159]**

        B: **has a VESTED REMAINDER, SUBJECT TO DIVESTMENT, in FEE SIMPLE ABSOLUTE**

        C: **has a SHIFTING EXECUTORY INEREST in FEE SIMPLE ABSOLUTE.**

---

[159] Whether the divesting condition would also cut short the life estate is beyond the scope of this introductory coverage.

ANSWERS TO PROBLEM SET 9

1.   O →   To A for life as long as A does not attend business school.

    A: **has a LIFE ESTATE DETERMINABLE**
    O: **has a REVERSION in FEE SIMPLE ABSOLUTE.**

2.   O →   To A for life as long as A does not attend business school, then to B and her heirs.

    A: **has a LIFE ESTATE DETERMINABLE**
    B: **has a VESTED REMAINDER in FEE SIMPLE ABSOLUTE.**

3.   O →   To A for life, but if A attends business school, then to B and her heirs.

    A: **has a LIFE ESTATE SUBJECT TO AN EXECUTORY INTEREST**
    B: **has a SHIFTING EXECUTORY INTERST in FEE SIMPLE ABSOLUTE**
    O: **has a REVERSION in FEE SIMPLE ABSOLUTE.**

ANSWERS TO PROBLEM SET 10

1.   O →   To A for life, then to A's heirs and their heirs.

    A: **has FEE SIMPLE ABSOLUTE.**

2.   O →   To A for life, then to O's heirs and their heirs.

    A: **has a LIFE ESTATE**
    O: **has a REVERSION in FEE SIMPLE ABSOLUTE.**

3.   O →   To A for life, then to O's heirs and their heirs one day after A's funeral.

    A: **has a LIFE ESTATE**
    O: **has a REVERSION in FEE SIMPLE ABSOLUTE.**

4.   O →   To A for life, then to B for life, then to the heirs of A's body and their heirs.

    A: **has a LIFE ESTATE**
    B: **has a VESTED REMAINDER in LIFE ESTATE**
    A: **has a VESTED REMAINDER in FEE TAIL.**
    O: **has a REVERSION in FEE SIMPLE ABSOLUTE.**

5.   O →   To A for life, then to A's heirs and their heirs one day after A's funeral

    A: **has a LIFE ESTATE**
    O: **has a REVERSION in FEE SIMPLE SUBJECT TO AN EXECUTORY LIMITATION**
A's HEIRS: **have a SPRINGING EXECUTORY INTEREST in FEE SIMPLE ABSOLUTE.**

ANSWERS TO PROBLEM SET 11

1.   O →   To A for life, then to A's children and their heirs.

(a) Assume A is alive and has no children.

A:	**has a LIFE ESTATE**
A's CHILDREN:	**have a CONTINGENT REMAINDER in FEE SIMPLE ABSOLUTE**
O:	**has a REVERSION IN FEE SIMPLE ABSOLUTE.**

(b) Assume A has a child B.

A:	**has a LIFE ESTATE**
A's CHILDREN:	**(B) have a VESTED REMAINDER, SUBJECT TO OPEN in FEE SIMPLE ABSOLUTE.**

(c) Assume B dies, survived by a child X.

A:	**has a LIFE ESTATE**
A's CHILDREN:	**(B) has a VESTED REMAINDER, SUBJECT TO OPEN in FEE SIMPLE ABSOLUTE (B's share, because it was vested, will descend to his or her heirs – X here).**

(d) Assume A has a second child C.

A:	**has a LIFE ESTATE**
A's CHILDREN:	**(B and C) have a VESTED REMAINDER, SUBJECT TO OPEN in FEE SIMPLE ABSOLUTE (B's share, because it was vested, will descend to his or her heirs – X).**

(e) Assume A dies.

B and C:	**hold the property in FEE SIMPLE ABSOLUTE (B's share because it was vested, descended to his or her heirs X – so X and C hold fee simple absolute).**

2.   O →   To A for life, then to B's children and their heirs.

    (a) Assume A is alive and B has no children.

A:	**has a LIFE ESTATE**
B's CHILDREN:	**have a CONTINGENT REMAINDER in FEE SIMPLE ABSOLUTE**
O:	**has a REVERSION IN FEE SIMPLE ABSOLUTE.**

    (b) Assume B has a child X.

A:	**has a LIFE ESTATE**
B's CHILDREN:	**(X) have a VESTED REMAINDER, SUBJECT TO OPEN in FEE SIMPLE ABSOLUTE.**

    (c) Assume B has a child Y.

A:	**has a LIFE ESTATE**
B's CHILDREN:	**(X and Y) have a VESTED REMAINDER, SUBJECT TO OPEN in FEE SIMPLE ABSOLUTE.**

    (d) Assume A dies, then B has a child Z.

X and Y:	**hold the property in FEE SIMPLE ABSOLUTE.**

ANSWERS TO REVIEW PROBLEM SET 12

1.   O →   To A and her heirs.

   A: holds a FEE SIMPLE ABSOLUTE.

2.   O →   To A forever, then to B forever, then to C and her heirs.

   (a) Common law:
   A: has a LIFE ESTATE
   B: has a VESTED REMAINDER in LIFE ESTATE
   C: has a VESTED REMAINDER in FEE SIMPLE
   ABSOLUTE.

   (b) Modern trend:
   Ambiguous, unclear how a court would resolve it. One approach would be to grant A a FEE SIMPLE ABSOLUTE and void all the other possible interest; the other would be to grant A a LIFE ESTATE, B a VESTED REMAINDER in LIFE ESTATE, and C a VESTED REMAINDER in FEE SIMPLE ABSOLUTE.

3.   O →   To A and the female heirs of her body, then to B in fee simple absolute, then to O and her heirs.

   (a) Common law:
   A: has a FEE TAIL FEMALE
   B: has a VESTED REMAINDER in LIFE ESTATE
   C: has a REVERSION IN FEE SIMPLE ABSOLUTE.

   (b) Modern trend (but not so modern as to have abolished the fee tail):
   Ambiguous, unclear how a court would resolve it. One approach would be to grant A a FEE TAIL FEMALE, B a VESTED REMAINDER IN FEE SIMPLE ABSOLUTE, and void the other possible interest in O; the other would be to grant A a FEE TAIL FEMALE, B a VESTED REMAINDER in LIFE ESTATE, and O a REVERSION in FEE SIMPLE ABSOLUTE.

4.   O → To A and her heirs as long as the land is used for agricultural purposes, then to Band her heirs.

   A: **has a FEE SIMPLE SUBJECT TO AN EXECUTORY LIMITATION**
   B: **has a SHIFTING EXECUTORY INTEREST in FEE SIMPLE ABSOLUTE.**

5.   O → To A and her heirs, but if A sells alcohol on the property, then X and her heirs shall have the right to enter and claim the land.

   A: **has a FEE SIMPLE SUBJECT TO AN EXECUTORY LIMITATION**
   X: **has a SHIFTING EXECUTORY INTEREST in FEE SIMPLE ABSOLUTE.**

6.   O → To A for life, then to B and her heirs if B graduates from medical school

   (a)   Assume A and B are alive.

   A: **has a LIFE ESTATE**
   B: **has a CONTINGETN REMAINDER in FEE SIMPLE ABSOLUTE**
   O: **has a REVERSION IN FEE SIMPLE ABSOLUTE.**

   (b) Assume A dies and B has not graduated from medical school.

   O: **has a FEE SIMPLE ABSOLUTE.**

7.   O → To A for life, then to B and her heirs if B graduates from medical school, otherwise to C and her heirs.

   (a) Assume A and B are alive.

   A: **has a LIFE ESTATE**
   B: **has a CONTINGENT REMAINDER in FEE SIMPLE ABSOLUTE**

C: **has an ALTERNATIVE CONTINGENT REMAINDER IN FEE SIMPLE ABSOLUTE**

O: **has a REVERSION IN FEE SIMPLE ABSOLUTE.**

(b-1) Assume A dies and B has not graduated from medical school.

C: **has a FEE SIMPLE ABSOLUTE.**

(b-2) Assume A renounces her interest and B has not graduated from medical school yet.

O: **has a FEE SIMPLE ABSOLUTE.**

(b-3) Assume B graduates from medical school, then B dies, and then A dies.

B: **has a FEE SIMPLE ABSOLUTE – B's interest is inheritable so it will pass to B's heirs.**

8. O → to A for life, then to B and her heirs if B attends A's funeral.

A: **has a LIFE ESTATE**

O: **has a REVERSION in FEE SIMPLE SUBJECT TO AN EXECUTORY LIMITATION**

B: **has a SPRINGING EXECUTORY INTEREST in FEE SIMPLE ABSOLUTE.**

9. O → To A for life, but if B graduates from medical school, then to B and her heirs.

A: **has a LIFE ESTATE SUBJECT TO AN EXECUTORY INTEREST**

B: **has a SHIFTING EXECUTORY INTEREST in FEE SIMPLE ABSOLUTE**

O: **has a REVERSION in FEE SIMPLE ABSOLUTE.**

10. O → To A for life, then to B and her heirs as long as B farms the land.

A: **has a LIFE ESTATE**

B: has a **VESTED REMINDER in FEE SIMPLE DETERMINABLE**

O: has a **POSSIBILITY OF REVERTER in FEE SIMPLE ABSOLUTE**

11.   O → To A for life, then to B and her heirs, but if B stops farming the land, then O may reenter and reclaim the land.

   A: has a **LIFE ESTATE**
   B: has a **VESTED REMAINDER in FEE SIMPLE SUBJECT TO A CONDITION SUBSEQUENT**
   O: has a **RIGHT OF ENTRY/POWER OF TERMINATION in FEE SIMPLE ABSOLUTE.**

12.   O → To A for life, then to B and her heirs, but if A stops farming the land, then to C and her heirs.

   A: has a **LIFE ESTATE**
   B: has a **VESTED REMAINDER, SUBJECT TO DIVESTMENT, in FEE SIMPLE ABSOLUTE**
   C: has a **SHIFTING EXECUTORY INTEREST in FEE SIMPLE ABSOLUTE.**

13.   O → To A for life, then to A's grandchildren and their heirs.

   (a) Assume A has no grandchildren.

   A: has a **LIFE ESTATE**
   A's GRANDCHILDREN: have a **CONTINGENT REMAINDER in FEE SIMPLE ABSOLUTE**
   O: has a **REVERSION IN FEE SIMPLE ABSOLUTE.**

   (b) Assume A has a grandchild X.

   A: has a **LIFE ESTATE**
   A's GRANDCHILDREN: (X) have a **VESTED REMAINDER, SUBJECT TO OPEN, in FEE SIMPLE ABSOLUTE**

(c) Assume A has another grandchild Y.

A: **has a LIFE ESTATE**
A's GRANDCHILDREN: **(X and Y) have a VESTED REMAINDER,**
     SUBJECT TO OPEN, in FEE SIMPLE
     ABSOLUTE

(d) assume X dies and then Y dies.

A: **has a LIFE ESTATE**
A's GRANDCHILDREN: **(X and Y) have a VESTED REMAINDER,**
     SUBJECT TO OPEN in FEE SIMPLE
     ABSOLUTE (their shares will pass to their
     heirs)

14.   O →   To A for life, then to B and her heirs as long as the land is farmed.

     A: **has a LIFE ESTATE**
     B: **has a VESTED REMAINDER in FEE SIMPLE**
     DETERMINABLE
     O: **has a POSSIBILITY OF REVERTER in FEE SIMPLE**
     ABSOLUTE.

15.   O →   To A for life, then to B and her heirs, but if B stops farming the land, then O can re-enter and reclaim the land.

     A: **has a LIFE ESTATE**
     B: **has a VESTED REMAINDER in FEE SIMPLE SUBJECT**
     TO A CONDITION SUBSEQUENT
     O: **has a RIGHT OF ENTRY in FEE SIMPLE ABSOLUTE.**

16.   O →   To A for life, then to B and her heirs as long as the land is farmed, then to C and her heirs.

     A: **has a LIFE ESTATE**
     B: **has a VESTED REMAINDER in FEE SIMPLE SUBJECT**
     TO AN
     EXECUTORY LIMITATION

    C: **has a SHIFTING EXECUTORY INTEREST in FEE SIMPLE ABSOLUTE**

17.   O →   To A for life, then to B and her heirs, but if B stops farming the land, then to C and her heirs.

    A: **has a LIFE ESTATE**
    B: **has a VESTED REMAINDER in FEE SIMPLE SUBJECT TO AN EXECUTORY LIMITATION**
    C: **has a SHIFTING EXECUTORY INTEREST in FEE SIMPLE ABSOLUTE.**

18.   O →   To A for life, then to B and her heirs, but if A stops farming the land, then to C and her heirs.

    A: **has a LIFE ESTATE**
    B: **has a VESTED REMAINDER, SUBJECT TO DIVESTMENT, in FEE SIMPLE ABSOLUTE**
    C: **has a SHIFTING EXECUTORY INTEREST in FEE SIMPLE ABSOLUTE.**

19.   O →   To A for life, then to B and her heirs, but if B marries C, then to X and her heirs.

(a) Assume A, B, C and X are alive.

    A: **has a LIFE ESTATE**
    B: **has a VESTED REMAINDER, SUBJECT TO DIVESTMENT, in FEE SIMPLE ABSOLUTE**
    C: **has a SHIFTING EXECUTORY INTEREST in FEE SIMPLE ABSOLUTE.**

(b) Assume A dies and B, C and X are alive.

    B: **has a FEE SIMPLE SUBJECT TO AN EXECUTORY LIMITATION**
    C: **has a SHIFTING EXECUTORY INTEREST in FEE SIMPLE ABSOLUTE.**

20.   O →   To A for life, then to B and her heirs if B graduates from law school.

(a) Assume A and B are both alive and B has not graduated from law school yet.

A: **has a LIFE ESTATE**
B: **has a CONTINGENT REMAINDER in FEE SIMPLE**
O: **has a REVERSION in FEE SIMPLE.**

21.   O →   To A for life, then to B and her heirs if B attends A's funeral.

A: **has a LIFE ESTATE**
O: **has a REVERSION in FEE SIMPLE SUBJECT TO AN EXECUTORY LIMITATION**
B: **has a SPRINGING EXECUTORY INTEREST in FEE SIMPLE ABSOLUTE.**

22.   O →   To A for life, then to B and her heirs if B graduates from law school.

(a) Assume A has died and B has not graduated from law school yet.

O: **has a FEE SIMPLE ABSOLUTE.**

23.   O →   To A for life, then to A's heirs and the heirs of their body.

A: **has a FEE TAIL**
O: **has a REVERSION in FEE SIMPLE ABSOLUTE.**

24.   O →   To A for life, then to B for life, then to A's heirs and the heirs of their body.

A: **has a LIFE ESTATE**
B: **has a VESTED REMAINDER in LIFE ESTATE**
A: **has a VESTED REMAINDER in FEE TAIL**
O: **has a REVERSION in FEE SIMPLE ABSOLUTE.**

25.   O →   To A for life, then to A's heirs and the heirs of their body if A
             survives B.

        A: **has a LIFE ESTATE**
        A: **has a CONTINGENT REMAINDER in FEE TAIL**
        O: **has a REVERSION in FEE SIMPLE ABSOLUTE.**

26.   O →   To A for life, then to A's heirs and their heirs who attend A's
             funeral.

        A: **has a LIFE ESTATE**
        O: **has a REVERSION in FEE SIMPLE SUBJECT TO AN
             EXECUTORY LIMITATION**
A's HEIRS: **have a SPRINGING EXECUTORY INTEREST in FEE
             SIMPLE ABSOLUTE.**

27.   O →   To A for life, then to O's heirs and the heirs of their body.

        A: **has a LIFE ESTATE**
        O: **has a REVERSION in FEE SIMPLE ABSOLUTE.**

28.   O →   To A for life, then to B for life, then to O's heirs and the heirs
             of their body.

        A: **has a LIFE ESTATE**
        B: **has a VESTED REMAINDER in LIFE ESTATE**
        O: **has a REVERSION in FEE SIMPLE ABSOLUTE.**

29.   O →   To A for life, then to O's heirs and the heirs of their body if A
             survives B.

        A: **has a LIFE ESTATE**
        O: **has a REVERSION in FEE SIMPLE ABSOLUTE.**

30.   O →   To A for life, then to A's heirs and their heirs if they spread
             A's ashes across the Pacific Ocean.

       A: **has a LIFE ESTATE**
       O: **has a REVERSION in FEE SIMPLE SUBJECT TO AN
               EXECUTORY LIMITATION**
A's HEIRS: **have a SPRINGING EXECUTORY INTEREST in FEE
               SIMPLE ABSOLUTE.**

31.   O →   To A for life as long as A does not attend medical school.

       A: **has a LIFE ESTATE DETERMINABLE**
       O: **has a REVERSION in FEE SIMPLE ABSOLUTE.**

32.   O →   To A for life as long as A does not attend medical school, then
             to B and her heirs.

       A: **has a LIFE ESTATE DETERMINABLE**
       B: **has a VESTED REMAINDER in FEE SIMPLE
               ABSOLUTE.**

33.   O →   To A for life, but if A attends medical school, then to B and her
             heirs.

       A: **has a LIFE ESTATE SUBJECT TO AN EXECUTORY
               LIMITATION**
       B: **has a SHIFTING EXECUTORY INTEREST in FEE
               SIMPLE ABSOLUTE**
       O: **has a REVERSION in FEE SIMPLE ABSOLUTE.**

PROBLEM SET 13

1.   O →   To A for life, then to B and her heirs if B reaches 25.

Assume B is 5.

A has a life estate, B has a contingent remainder in fee simple, and O has a reversion in fee simple. Put B's contingent remainder to the test:

   1. Create: A new life in being X, an heir for B.
   2. Kill: O, A and B.
   3. Count 21 yrs: Can you create a scenario in which a new life in being will be able to claim the property under the interest in question but only after the lives in being plus 21 years has passed?

   No. Because the remainder will vest only if B reaches age 25, there is no way to satisfy the condition but after the lives in being plus 21 years. Because we could not create a scenario in which the contingent remainder vests, but only after the lives in being plus 21 years, the contingent remainder is valid.

2.   O →   To A for life, then to A's first child and his or her heirs.

Assume A has no children yet.

   1. Create: A new life in being, X, a child for A.
   2. Kill: O and A.
   3. Count 21 years: Can you create a scenario in which a new life in being will be able to claim the property under the interest in question but only after the lives in being plus 21 years has passed?

   No. The contingent remainder in A's first child will vest immediately upon the creation of the first child, X, and there is no way to delay the vesting until after the lives in being plus 21 years. Therefore, the contingent remainder is valid.

3.   O →   To A for life, then to A's first child to reach age 30 and his or her heirs.

Assume A has 2 children: B, age 25, and C, age 28.

A has a life estate, A's first child to reach age 30 has a contingent remainder in fee simple and O has a reversion in fee simple. Put the contingent remainder A's first child to reach age 30 holds to the test:

1. **Create: A new life in being, X, a new child for A.**
2. **Kill: O, A, B and C.**
3. **Count 21 yrs: Can you create a scenario in which a new life in being will be able to claim the property under the interest in question but only after the lives in being plus 21 years have passed?**

    Yes. Is it possible that X will live for another 9 years and reach age 30, at which time the contingent remainder will vest. Because the contingent remainder vested under this scenario after the lives in being plus 21 years, the contingent remainder is invalid.

4.   O →   To A for life, then to A's first child to reach age 21 and his or her heirs.

Assume A has 2 children: B, age 19, and C, age 18.

A has a life estate, A's first child to reach age 21 has a contingent remainder in fee simple, and O has a reversion in fee simple. Put the contingent remainder A's first child to reach age 21 holds to the test:

1. **Create: A new life in being, X, a new child for A.**
2. **Kill: O, A, B and C.**
3. **Count 21 yrs: Can you create a scenario in which a new life in being will be able to claim the property under the interest in question but only after the lives in being plus 21 years has passed?**

No. X will reach age 21 before the lives in being plus 21 years has expired. There is no way to delay the vesting until after the lives in being plus 21 years. There fore, the contingent remainder is valid.

5.   O → To A for life, then to A's first grandchild and his or her heirs.

Assume A has 6 children and no grandchildren.

A has a life estate, A's first grandchild has a contingent remainder in fee simple, and O has a reversion in fee simple. Put the contingent remainder A's first grandchild holds to the test:

1. Create: A new life in being, X, a new CHILD for A (create as far back as possible).
2. Kill: O, A, B and C.
3. Count 21 yrs: Can you create a scenario in which a new life in being will be able to claim the property under the interest in question but only after the lives in being plus 21 years has passed?

   Yes. It is conceivable that X can have a child who would be A's first grandchild, which would vest the remainder but after the lives in being plus 21 years. Therefore, the contingent remainder is invalid.

6.   O devises Greenacres to A for life, then to O's first grandchild and his or her heirs.

O has no grandchildren yet, but 5 children.

A has a life estate, O's first grandchild has a contingent remainder in fee simple, and O has a reversion in fee simple. Put the contingent remainder O's first grandchild holds to the test:

1. **Create: A new life in being, X, O's new GRANDCHILD.**
2. **Kill: A and the 5 children.**
3. **Count 21 yrs: Can you create a scenario in which a new life in being will be able to claim the property under the interest in question but only after the lives in being plus 21 years has passed?**

No. Because this conveyance is by will ("devise" indicates the transfer is by will), O is deceased so we cannot create another child for O. The only person we can create is a grandchild for O, which immediately vests the remainder. There is no way to delay the vesting until after the lives in being plus 21 years. Therefore, the contingent remainder is valid.

7.   O → To A for life, then to B's first child to graduate from law school and his or her heirs. Assume B has two children, and one of them is second year law student.

A has a life estate, B's first child to graduate from law school has a contingent remainder in fee simple, and O has a reversion in fee simple. Put the contingent remainder B's first child to graduate from law school holds to the test:

1. **Create: A new life in being, X, a new child for B.**
2. **Kill: O, A, B and B's two children.**
3. **Count 21 yrs: Can you create a scenario in which a new life in being will be able to claim the property under the interest in question but only after the lives in being plus 21 years has passed?**

   Yes. It is conceivable that after the lives in being plus 21 years that X will go and graduate from law school. Therefore, the contingent remainder is invalid.

8.   O → To A for life, then to A's widow for life, then to A's children who survive A's widow and their heirs.

A has a life estate, A's widow has a contingent remainder for life, and A's children who survive A's widow have a contingent

remainder in fee simple, and O has a reversion in fee simple.

(A) Put the contingent remainder A's widow holds to the test:

1. **Create: A new life in being, X, who marries A.**
2. **Kill: O and A.**
3. **Count 21 yrs: Can you create a scenario in which a new life in being will be able to claim the property under the interest in question but only after the lives in being plus 21 years has passed?**

    No. The contingent remainder in A's widow will vest immediately upon A's death. There is no way to delay the vesting until after the lives in being plus 21 years. Therefore, the contingent remainder in A's children who survive A's widow is invalid.

(B) Put the contingent remainder A's children who survive A's widow hold to the test:

1. **Create: A new life in being, X, who A marries, and then Y, a child of A.**
2. **Kill: O and A.**
3. **Count 21 yrs: Can you create a scenario in which a new life in being will be able to claim the property under the interest in question but only after the lives in being plus 21 years has passed?**

    Yes, after the lives in being plus 21 years, X (A's widow) dies, at which time the contingent remainder in A's children who survive A's widow vests. Therefore, the contingent remainder in A's children who survive A's widow is invalid.

9.   O →   To A for life, then to A's widow for life, then to A's children and their heirs.

A has a life estate, A's widow has a contingent remainder for life, and A's children who survive A's widow have a contingent remainder in fee simple, and O has a reversion in fee simple.

(A) Put the contingent remainder A's widow holds to the test:

1. **Create: A new life in being, X, who marries A.**
2. **Kill: O and A.**
3. **Count 21 yrs: Can you create a scenario in which a new life in being will be able to claim the property under the interest in question but only after the lives in being plus 21 years has passed?**

    No. The contingent remainder in A's widow will vest immediately upon A's death. There is no way to delay the vesting until after the lives in being plus 21 years. Therefore, the contingent remainder in A's children who survive A's widow is invalid.

(B) Put the contingent remainder A's children hold to the test:

1. **Create: A new life in being, X, whom A marries, and then Y, child of A..**
2. **Kill: O and A.**
3. **Count 21 yrs: Can you create a scenario in which a new life in being will be able to claim the property under the interest in question but only after the lives in being plus 21 years has passed?**

    No. The contingent remainder in A's children will vest upon the creation of A's child Y and there is no scenario in which a child can vest in the interest but only after the lives in being plus 21 years. Therefore, the contingent remainder is valid.

PROBLEM SET 14

1.   O →   To A and her heirs as long as the land is used for
               educational purposes; and if it is not used for educational
               purposes, then to B and her heirs.

**A holds a fee simple subject to an executory limitation, and B
holds a shifting executory interest in fee simple. Put B's
executory interest to the test:**

1. **Create: A new life in being: X, an heir for A and Y an heir
    for B.**
2. **Kill: O, A and B.**
3. **Count 21 yrs: Can you create a scenario in which a new life
    in being will be able to claim the property under the interest
    in question but only after the lives in being plus 21 years
    have passed?**

    **Yes. It is conceivable that after the lives in being plus 21
    years A's heir, X, will stop using the land for educational
    purposes and B's heir, Y, will be entitled to claim possession
    of the land under the executory interest. Because the
    executory interest could become possessory after the lives in
    being plus 21 years, the interest is invalid.**

2.   O →   to whoever is the President of Pepperdine University at the
               time of distribution of my estate and his or her heirs.

**O has a fee simple subject to an executory limitation, and
whoever is the President of Pepperdine University at the time
O's estate is distributed holds a springing executory interest in
fee simple. Put the executory interest to the test:**

1. **Create: A new life in being: X, a new President for
    Pepperdine University, and Y, a personal representative to
    distribute O's estate.**
2. **Kill: O and all the other lives in being at the time the
    interest was created.**
3. **Count 21 yrs: Can you create a scenario in which a new life
    in being will be able to claim the property under the interest**

in question but only after the lives in being plus 21 years has passed?

Yes. It is conceivable that Y will be slow in distributing O's estate and it will not occur until after the lives in being plus 21 years. Therefore, the executory interest is invalid.

3.   O →   To A for life, then to B and her heirs, but if B ever sells liquor on the land, to C and her heirs.

A has a life estate, B has a vested remainder in fee simple subject to an executory limitation, and C has a shifting executory interest in fee simple. Put C's executory interest to the test:

1. Create: A new life in being: X, an heir for B, and Y, an heir for C.
2. Kill: A, B and C.
3. Count 21 yrs: Can you create a scenario in which a new life in being will be able to claim the property under the interest in question but only after the lives in being plus 21 years has passed?

No. C's executory interest can only become possessory if B sells liquor on the land. Once we kill B, there is no way the condition can occur 21 years later. Therefore, the executory interest is valid.

PROBLEM SET 15

1.   O →   To A for life, then to A's children and their heirs.

(a). Assume A has no children.

A has a life estate, A's children have a contingent remainder in fee simple, and O has a reversion. Put the contingent remainder A's children hold to the test:

1. **Create: A new life in being: X, a child for A.**
2. **Kill: O and A.**
3. **Count 21 yrs: Can you conceive of a scenario in which the new member of the class, X, will vest in the property but only after the lives in being plus 21 years?**

> **No. X will vest in his or her interest the moment he or she is born. There is no way to delay X's vesting until after the lives in being plus 21 years. Therefore, the contingent remainder is valid.**

(b) Assume A has a child, X.

A has a life estate, A's children have a vested remainder, subject to open, in fee simple, and O has a reversion. Put the vested remainder subject to open A's children hold to the test:

1. **Create: A new life in being: Y, a new child for A.**
2. **Kill: O, A and X.**
3. **Count 21 yrs: Can you conceive of a scenario in which, Y, the new member of the class, will vest in the property but only after the lives in being plus 21 years?**

> **No. Y will vest in his or her interest the moment he or she is born. There is no way to delay Y's vesting until after the lives in being plus 21 years. Therefore, the vested remainder subject to open is valid.**

(c) Assume A dies.

X holds fee simple absolute.

2.   O → to A for life, then to B's children and their heirs.

(a) Assume B has no children.

A has a life estate, B's children have a contingent remainder in fee simple, and O has a reversion. Put the contingent remainder B's children hold to the test:

1. **Create:** A new life in being: X, a child for B.
2. **Kill:** O, A and B.
3. **Count 21 yrs:** Can you conceive of a scenario in which the new member of the class, X, will vest in the property but only after the lives in being plus 21 years?

     No. X will vest in his or her interest the moment he or she is born. There is no way to delay X's vesting until after the lives in being plus 21 years. Therefore, the contingent remainder is valid.

(b) Assume B has a child, X.

A has a life estate, B's children have a vested remainder, subject to open, in fee simple, and O has a reversion. Put the vested remainder to open B's children hold to the test:

1. **Create:** A new life in being: Y, a child for B.
2. **Kill:** O, A, B and X.
3. **Count 21 yrs:** Can you conceive of a scenario in which the new member of the class, Y, the new member of the class, will vest in the property but only after the lives in being plus 21 years?

     No. Y will vest in his or her interest the moment he or she is born. There is no way to delay Y's vesting until after the lives in being plus 21 years. Therefore, the contingent remainder is valid.

(c) Assume A dies.

X holds fee simple absolute. Even though B is still alive, under the Rule of Convenience, the class closes the moment one member of the class is entitled to actual possession. The moment A died, the vested remainder subject to open became possessory, thereby closing the class.

(d) Assume B has a child, Y.

X holds fee simple absolute. Even though B is still alive and had another child Y, under the Rule of Convenience, the class closes the moment one member of the class is entitled to actual possession. The moment A died, the vested remainder subject to open became possessory, thereby closing the class. Y has no right to claim an interest in the property.

3.   O →   To A for life, then to A's grandchildren and their heirs.
            A has no grandchildren yet.

A has a life estate, A's grandchildren have a contingent remainder in fee simple, and O has a reversion in fee simple. Put the contingent remainder A's grandchildren hold to the test.

1. **Create: A new life in being: X, a CHILD for A (create as far back as possible).**
2. **Kill: O and A.**
3. **Count 21 yrs: Can you conceive of a scenario in which the contingent remainder will vest in a class member but only after the lives in being plus 21 years?**

    Yes. After the lives in being plus 21 years, X could have a child Y, A's first grandchild. The remainder would vest in Y, but after the lives in being plus 21 years. Therefore, the contingent remainder is invalid.

4.   O →   To A for life, then to A's children who reach age 21 and his or her heirs.

Assume A has 2 children: X, age 25; and Y, age 5.

A has a life estate, A's children who reach age 21 have a vested remainder subject to open in fee simple, and O has a reversion. Put the vested remainder subject to open A's children who reach age 21 hold to the test:

1. Create: A new life in being: Z, a new child for A.
2. Kill: O, A, X and Y.
3. Count 21 yrs: Can you conceive of a scenario in which the new member of the class, Z, will vest in the property but only after the lives in being plus 21 years?

   No. Z will vest in his or her interest the moment he or she turns 21 which must occur before the lives in being plus 21 years has passed. There is no way to delay X's vesting until after the lives in being plus 21 years. Because we cannot create a scenario in which a class member vests but only after the lives in being plus 21 years the vested remainder subject to open is valid.

5.   O → To A for life, then to B's children who reach age 25 and his or her heirs.

Assume B has a child, X, age 27.

A has a life estate, B's children who reach age 25 have a vested remainder subject to open in fee simple, and O has a reversion. Put the vested remainder subject to open B's children who reach age 25 hold to the test:

1. Create: A new life in being: Z, a new child for B.
2. Kill: O, A, and X.
3. Count 21 yrs: Can you conceive of a scenario in which the new member of the class, Z, will vest in the property but only after the lives in being plus 21 years?

   Yes. Z will not vest in his or her interest until he or she turns 21 which must occur after the lives in being plus 21 years has passed. Although A's death closes the class, Z is already in the class but not vested because of the express condition precedent: that the class members must reach age 25. Because we have created a scenario in which a class member vests in his or her interest but not until after the lives in being plus 21 years, the vested remainder subject to open is invalid.

Subject Matter Index